## About Island Press

Island Press is the only nonprofit organization in the United States whose principal purpose is the publication of books on environmental issues and natural resource management. We provide solutions-oriented information to professionals, public officials, business and community leaders, and concerned citizens who are shaping responses to environmental problems.

In 1994, Island Press celebrated its tenth anniversary as the leading provider of timely and practical books that take a multidisciplinary approach to critical environmental concerns. Our growing list of titles reflects our commitment to bringing the best of an expanding body of literature to the environmental community throughout North America and the world.

Support for Island Press is provided by Apple Computer, Inc., The Bullitt Foundation, The Geraldine R. Dodge Foundation, The Energy Foundation, The Ford Foundation, The W. Alton Jones Foundation, The Lyndhurst Foundation, The John D. and Catherine T. MacArthur Foundation, The Andrew W. Mellon Foundation, The Joyce Mertz-Gilmore Foundation, The National Fish and Wildlife Foundation, The Pew Charitable Trusts, The Pew Global Stewardship Initiative, The Rockefeller Philanthropic Collaborative, Inc., and individual donors.

# ECOLOGICAL DESIGN

# ECOLOGICAL
# DESIGN

*Sim Van der Ryn*

*and Stuart Cowan*

ISLAND PRESS

*Washington, D.C.* • *Covelo, California*

ISLAND PRESS is a trademark of The Center for Resource Economics.

Figures 1–3 and 9–18 by Peter Calagero. Figures 4–6 and 19–24 courtesy of
Ecological Design Institute. Figures 7 and 8 courtesy of the California
Office of the State Architect.

Library of Congress Cataloging in Publication Data

Van der Ryn. Sim.
      Ecological design / Sim Van der Ryn and Stuart Cowan.
            p.   cm.
      Includes bibliographical references and index.
      ISBN 1-55963-388-3 (cloth: alk. paper).—ISBN 1-55963-389-1
(paper : alk. paper)
      1. Environmental policy.   2. Human ecology.   3. Social ecology.
4. Biodiversity.   I. Cowan, Stuart, 1965–   .   II. Title.
      GE170.V36   1996                                   95-20700
      363.7—dc20                                         CIP

Printed on recycled, acid-free paper ∞

Manufactured in the United States of America

10 9 8 7 6 5 4 3 2 1

# CONTENTS

# PREFACE

If we are to create a sustainable world—one in which we are accountable to the needs of all future generations and all living creatures—we must recognize that our present forms of agriculture, architecture, engineering, and technology are deeply flawed. To create a sustainable world, we must transform these practices. We must infuse the design of products, buildings, and landscapes with a rich and detailed understanding of ecology.

Sustainability needs to be firmly grounded in the nitty-gritty details of design. Policies and pronouncements have their place, but ultimately we must address specific *design* problems: How can we design our products and manufacturing processes so that materials are completely reclaimed? How can we create wastewater treatment systems that enhance, rather than damage, their surrounding ecosystems? How can we design buildings that produce their own energy and recycle their own wastes? How can we create agricultural systems that are not dependent on subsidies of pesticides, fertilizers, and fossil fuels?

Design problems like these bridge conventional scientific and design disciplines. They can be solved only if industrial designers talk to biogeochemists, sanitation engineers to wetland biologists, architects to physicists, and farmers to ecologists. In order to successfully integrate ecology and design, we must mirror nature's deep interconnections in our own epistemology of design. We are still trapped in worn-out mechanical metaphors. It is time to stop designing in the image of the machine and start designing in a way that honors the complexity and diversity of life itself.

This is a book about *ecological design,* which can be defined as "any form of design that minimizes environmentally destructive impacts by integrating itself with living processes." Ecological design is an integrative, ecologically responsible design discipline. It helps connect scattered efforts in green architecture, sustainable agriculture, ecological engineering, and other fields. Ecological design is both a profoundly hopeful vision and a pragmatic tool. By placing ecology in the foreground of design, it provides specific ways of minimizing energy and materials use, reducing pollution, preserving habitat, and fostering community, health, and beauty. It provides a new way of *thinking about* design.

This book emerges from two voices spanning several generations. One of us has spent more than thirty years practicing, teaching, and exploring ecological design. The other, trained in science and mathematics, and with an equally strong love for the natural world, is not yet thirty. Our respective worlds of architecture and nonlinear dynamics meet in what Wendell Berry calls "searching for pattern." The following pages took form out of our dialogues devoted to this search. They exemplify the kind of interdisciplinary dialogue that we feel is central to ecological design.

This book is not a design handbook or a technical reference filled with detailed case studies, charts, and tables. These details are vitally important, but our concern here is to give them context and connect them into a coherent whole. This book grows from the conviction that people in very different design disciplines are beginning to struggle with the same questions. Both automobile designers and architects are looking at the entire life-cycle of the materials they choose and are designing in ways that allow these materials to be reclaimed. Landscape architects and environmental engineers are working together to create artificial wetlands to purify wastewater. Responding to this shared quest, this book is a small step toward creating a design process that has the preservation and restoration of the ecological commons at its core.

The first part of the book, "Bringing Design to Life," presents an overview of ecological design. The first chapter discusses the connection between sustainability and design. The second chapter is a self-contained statement of the underlying principles and philosophy of ecological design, concluding with a short history of the field. "Nature's Geometry," the third chapter, suggests that we look for design principles that explicitly link different levels of scale from the molecular to the planetary.

The book's second part, "The Ecological Design Process," devotes chapters to five design principles that we think are fundamental to ecological design. These principles are intended as a starting point, an inspiration to creativity rather than a definitive set of rules.

The book concludes with a resource guide and an annotated bibliography for those wishing to explore these concepts further. The resource guide provides current contact information for some of the most interesting projects and organizations in the field of ecological design. The bibliography describes books that have been critical to our thinking and to the development of ecological design.

Our discussions are, of necessity, incomplete. There is an extraordinary proliferation of excellent work in ecological design, and it would take dozens of volumes to treat it fully. Instead of striving for completeness, we chose examples that best demonstrate the patterns of thought involved in ecological design. As a result, some fields with a great deal of significant activity—particularly renewable energy, transportation, and urban planning—are not well represented.

This book would not have been possible without the extraordinary contributions of our predecessors and contemporaries. In turn, it is offered to the next generation in a spirit of hope.

*Sim Van der Ryn and Stuart Cowan*

# ACKNOWLEDGMENTS

I owe a great deal to my students in ecological design seminars and studios at the University of California at Berkeley. Over the years their enthusiasm, questioning, and commitment to finding a better design path was a constant source of emotional support, friendship, and intellectual stimulation.

The Lindisfarne Association has long been an intellectual family to me. William Irwin Thompson, its founder, and the Fellows have been mentors, soulmates, and constant sources of inspiration. My thanks to Beatrice Thompson, John and Nancy Todd, Wes and Dana Jackson, Mary Catherine Bateson, Lois Bateson, Gary Snyder, Wendell Berry, Fritz and Vivienne Hull, Amory and Hunter Lovins, Lynn Margulis, Robert and Ellen McDermott, Robert Thurman, Richard Baker, and Joan Halifax.

My work family at the Ecological Design Institute has always accepted my irregular schedule and preoccupations with patience and good humor. Thanks especially to Peter Retondo, David Arkin, and Marci Riseman. Conversations with Michael Katz, Christine Price, David Harris, and Cherie Forrester were helpful in shaping the book. The board of the Ecological Design Institute—Marty Krasney, Ranny Riley, and Michael Murphy—has always supported my vision with good cheer and sound advice.

Stuart Cowan enrolled in my ecological design seminar in 1992 and brought a fresh perspective and keen intelligence to the class. A book had been taking shape in my mind and on paper for some time. I invited Stuart to collaborate with me, and through several years of long talks and rambling walks through the forests and beaches of Point Reyes my shapeless notes emerged into a new form from our joint efforts. It's been a pleasure to be in the company of his upbeat temperament, energetic metabolism, and quick mind.

Finally, thanks to my wife and partner, Ruth Friend, who generously created space for the process of writing this book, and who always reminds me through our life and hers what the point of all of this is.

*Sim Van der Ryn*

This book would have been impossible to write without the constant care and compassion of my wife, Katy Langstaff. A fine ecological designer and builder, she has challenged me to feel more deeply and write more clearly. Her voice and spirit inform every page. Without her courage, I would have given up on this book long ago.

I am also greatly indebted to my coauthor, Sim Van der Ryn, who took a chance on an eccentric young mathematician more than two years ago. Sim has been an extraordinary mentor and friend during a critical turning point in my life. Thanks for the bocce ball tournaments, clam chowder, and hikes.

I'd like to thank my parents for their love and support, and for the opportunity to grow up with mountain, forest, and ocean companions. Thanks to Moe Hirsch, Richard Norgaard, and Leigh Palmer, three teachers of great integrity who have deeply influenced my path. Robin Grossinger and Elise Brewster have been greatly valued symbionts in the collective we call Lichen. Thanks also to the Archipelago group—Fernando Marti, Andrea Cowles, and Norm Bourassa—for some wonderful times and much-needed support. Thanks to our patient editor, Fran

Haselsteiner, for turning an amorphous first draft into a much more focused text. And many thanks to those friends who have provided a nourishing context for a difficult book, including David Austin, Ann Baker, Rebecca Boone, Rebecca Coffman, Nelson Denman, Nicole Egger, Francis Frick, Helen Hoyer, Fritz and Vivienne Hull, Aran Kaufer, Richard Kraft, Penny Livingston, Allison and Jenn Rader, Sarah Smith, James Stark, James Stone, Joanne Tippet, Babak Tondre, John and Nancy Todd, and Micah Van der Ryn.

*Stuart Cowan*

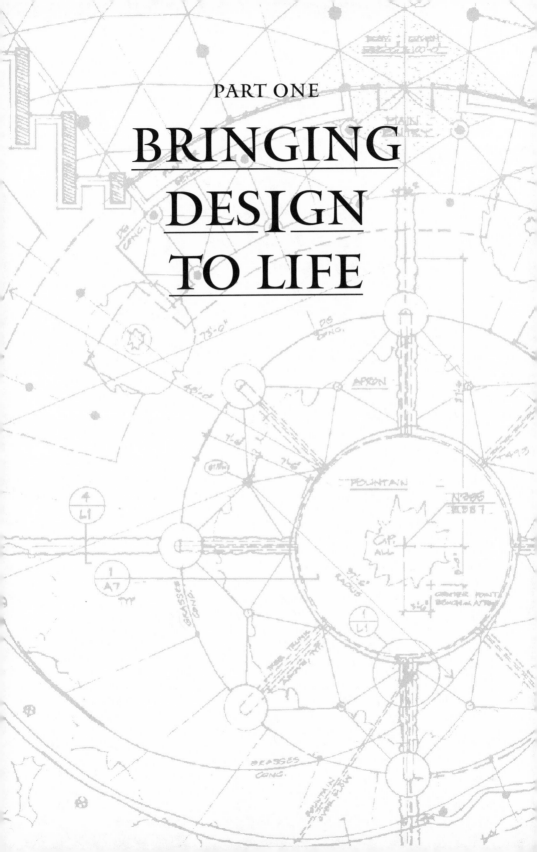

PART ONE

# BRINGING
# DESIGN
# TO LIFE

# SUSTAINABILITY
# AND DESIGN

## TWO VIEWS OF SUSTAINABILITY

The word *sustainability* has become a kind of mantra for the 1990s, offering the possibility of balance and permanence in a world where we experience precisely the opposite. Today, our rapid exploitation of fossil fuels is already changing climate patterns so catastrophically that many insurance companies will no longer insure against extreme weather events. One hundred square miles of rainforest are being lost each day. Species are going extinct at the unprecedented rate of three per hour. Chemicals once thought relatively harmless to humans are turning out to affect immune and endocrine systems. The list of environmental damage is endless, from the depleted soils of the cornbelt to the vast industrial disaster zones of Eastern Europe and the former Soviet Union. In search of comfort, convenience, and material wealth, we have begun to sacrifice not only our own health, but also the health of all species. We are starting to exhaust the capacity of the very systems that sustain us, and now we must deal with the consequences.

In this context, the emergence of the sustainability movement is deeply inspiring, for it potentially offers a holistic response to the environmental crisis that makes much-needed connections between nature, culture, values, power relationships, and technology. In the face of overwhelming change, sustainability is an idea that absorbs our genuine hope to create cultures and places with enough integrity to persist for our grandchildren and beyond.

A huge literature on sustainability has developed over the past ten years, offering analysis after analysis of the lack of sustainability in both the Northern and Southern Hemispheres. Various underlying causes are invoked, including capitalism, Christianity, colonialism, development, the population explosion, science and technology, and patriarchal culture.[1] These diagnoses are valuable, and all have considerable merit, yet they largely fail to deliver the particulars involved in making the transition to a more sustainable world. Instead, we are left with hopeful, but vague, policy statements.

Sustainability is not a single movement or approach. It is as varied as the communities and interests currently grappling with the issues it raises. The shape that it will take is being contested now, and the stakes are high. On the one hand, sustainability is the province of global policymakers and environmental experts flying at thirty-five thousand feet from conference to conference. On the other hand, sustainability is also the domain of grassroots environmental and social groups, indigenous peoples preserving traditional practices, and people committed to changing their own communities.

The environmental educator David W. Orr calls these two approaches *technological sustainability* and *ecological sustainability*. While both are coherent responses to the environmental crisis, they are far apart in their specifics. Technological sustainability, which seems to get most of the airtime, may be characterized this way: "Every problem has either a technological answer or a market solution. There are no dilemmas to be avoided, no domains where angels fear to tread."[2] It is about expert interventions in which the planet's medical symptoms are carefully stabilized through high-profile international agreements and sophisticated management techniques. Ecological sustainability, in contrast, "is the task of finding alternatives to the practices that got us into trouble in the first place; it is necessary to rethink agriculture, shelter, energy use, urban design, transportation, economics, community patterns, resource use, forestry, the importance of wilderness, and our central values."[3] While the two approaches have important points of contact, including a shared awareness of the extent of the global environmental crisis, they embody two very different visions of a sustainable society.

The proponents of technological sustainability assert that a fundamental change in direction is not necessary. For an example of this approach we need look no further than the highly influential 1987 report of the World Commission on Environment and Development, *Our Common Future*. According to the report, "Sustainable development is development that meets the needs of the present without compromising the ability of future generations to meet their own needs."[4] This definition is bland but superficially appealing, for it at least makes reference to the future inhabitants of the planet. It is deliberately phrased as unobtrusively as possible. Unfortunately, it begs a number of critical questions: What constitutes a need? Given our uncertainties about living systems, can we guarantee that this generation's actions will still leave viable ecosystems for future generations?

On reading *Our Common Future* more carefully, we find that sustainability is to be attained by "more rapid economic growth in both industrial and developing countries, freer market access for the products of developing countries, lower interest rates, greater technology transfer, and significantly larger capital flows."[5] This prescription implies a highly technical approach based on more and better management and technology.

A generation ago, many of society's most powerful voices denied any alternative to a cornucopian spiral of material, technological, and economic expansion. Now these same voices seem to be embracing sustainability and sustainable development—terms that suggest the acceptance of limits and the recognition that our material wealth and physical well-being depend on nature's own health. Has the underlying assumption that everything can be measured and controlled changed, or has our hubris simply expanded to include the notion that we can manage all of nature in a way that is "more sustainable"? Is technological sustainability simply a kinder, gentler form of reductionism in which we do a more efficient job of using up, accounting for, and managing nature?

Some very disturbing assumptions lurk behind the utopian vision of sustainability via global ecological management. We need to question both our choice of managers and the knowledge informing the managers' decisions. The development critic Wolfgang Sachs observes that the satellite images so critical to global environmental management construct

> a reality that contains mountains of data, but no people. The data do not explain why the Tuaregs are driven to exhaust their water-holes, or what makes Germans so obsessed with high speed on freeways; they do not point out who owns the timber shipped from the Amazon or which industry flourishes because of a polluted Mediterranean sea; and they are mute about the significance of forest trees for Indian tribals or what water means to an Arab country. In short, they provide a knowledge which is faceless and placeless; an abstraction that carries a considerable cost: it consigns the realities of culture, power and virtue to oblivion.[6]

One reason technological sustainability is compelling is that it seems to fit well into existing structures of power. "Sustainable development" is already being used to justify a wide variety of conventional large-scale development schemes. In the case of the Narmada Dam project in India, this language has been invoked to justify the forced dislocation of tens of thousands of traditional villagers so that electricity may become marginally cheaper for urban dwellers and huge industrial customers. According to a recent article in *The Ecologist,* "Both those resisting and those defending the Narmada Valley Project use the language of social justice and sustainable development, and both lobbies have justified their stance with cost-benefit analyses and grassroots mobilization."[7] Technological sustainability looks to a new group of experts to fine-tune the global interface between people and the biosphere, and in the process, it often neglects the details of culture and community while displaying a rather naive optimism concerning our ability to manage planetary systems.

Ecological sustainability, in contrast, embraces assumptions very different from the thinly veiled business-as-usual optimism of *Our Common Future*. It requires limits to technology, limits to material wants, limits to the stress placed on the biosphere, and limits to hubris.

Four of David W. Orr's characteristics of ecological sustainability are worth summarizing here.[8] First, people are finite and fallible. The human ability to comprehend and manage scale and complexity has limits. Thinking too big can make our human limitations a liability rather than an asset. Second, a sustainable world can be redesigned and rebuilt only from the bottom up. Locally self-reliant and self-organized communities are the building blocks for change. Third, traditional knowledge that co-evolves out of culture and place is a critical asset. It needs to be preserved, restored, and used. Fourth, the true harvest of evolution is encoded in nature's design. Nature is more than a bank of resources to draw on: it is the best model we have for all the design problems we face.

These characteristics imply that the only long-term approach to building a sustainable world is to redesign the details of the products, buildings, and landscapes around us. Such redesign—attending carefully to scale, community self-reliance, traditional knowledge, and the wisdom of nature's own designs—requires patience and humility. It is a search for the nitty-gritty design details of a sustainable culture, one grounded in the texture of our everyday lives.

### THE DESIGN CONNECTION

The most significant change in architecture over the last century has been the growing dependence of homes on centralized technological infrastructures for the provision of food, fuel, water, and building materials. . . . One BTU in twelve of world energy production is used to heat and cool the U.S. building stock. . . . On average it takes as much energy to heat and cool the U.S. building stock for three years as it took to build it in the first place. Home furnaces are the largest source of air pollution after automobiles. . . . An average house uses between 150 and 200 gallons of water per inhabitant per day. . . . All water used in buildings, no matter for what purpose, exits as sewage. Our water and sewage systems are coupled in series. We quite literally defecate in our water systems in the name of personal hygiene. . . . The average home produces 4.5 pounds of garbage per person per day, or anywhere from 2.5 to 5 tons per year. Fibers, plastics, paper, wood, glass, metal and food scraps are usually all thrown in the same trash bin. A lot of highly organized materials in the input channels are combined in one "noisy" exit channel and dumped; disorder or entropy is maximized.

SEAN WELLESLEY-MILLER, "Towards a Symbiotic Architecture"[9]

For our purposes, let us define *design* as the intentional shaping of matter, energy, and process to meet a perceived need or desire. Design is a hinge that inevitably connects culture and nature through exchanges of materials, flows of energy, and choices of land use. By this definition, architects, landscape architects, and city planners are clearly designers, but so are farmers, chemical engineers, industrial designers, interior decorators, and many others. All are involved in shaping the physical details of our daily experience.

The everyday world of buildings, artifacts, and domesticated landscapes is a designed world, one shaped by human purpose. The physical form of this world is a direct manifestation of what is most valued in our culture. According to this criterion, the complex array of information needed to build a skyscraper counts as valid knowledge while the equally sophisticated information needed to grow food without pesticides may not. Philosophers call a filter that determines what counts as knowledge an *epistemology*. Tomatoes, flush toilets, cars, nuclear-power plants, culverts, and suburbs each embody an epistemology in which environmental concerns may or may not play an explicit role. By eating a tomato, flushing the toilet, driving a car, or turning on a light we are drawn into the corresponding epistemology.

In many ways, the environmental crisis is a design crisis. It is a consequence of how things are made, buildings are constructed, and landscapes are used. Design manifests culture, and culture rests firmly on the foundation of what we believe to be true about the world. Our present forms of agriculture, architecture, engineering, and industry are derived from design epistemologies incompatible with nature's own. It is clear that we have not given design a rich enough context. We have used design cleverly in the service of narrowly defined human interests but have neglected its relationship with our fellow creatures. Such myopic design cannot fail to degrade the living world, and, by extension, our own health.

If we believe we can sever our design decisions from their ecological consequences, we will design accordingly. We will consistently find, in the words of Wendell Berry, a "solution that causes a ramifying series of new problems, the only limiting criterion being, apparently, that the new problems should arise beyond the purview of the expertise that produced the solution."[10] Thus, while pesticides may partially curb the immediate problem—an abundance of pests—they often create a chain of new problems left unconsidered by those who design pesticides. These problems are large and diffuse, including the exposure of farmworkers to carcinogens, polluted groundwater, and impacts on the beneficial birds and insects that might have kept the pests in check in the first place.

Over the past fifty years, we have reduced a complex and diverse landscape into an asphalt network stitched together from coast to coast out of a dozen or so crude design "templates." The poverty of the industrial imagination is manifested in the limited number of templates used to meet every imaginable need. There are strip malls, mini-malls, regional malls, industrial parks, edge cities, detached single-family homes, townhouses, and sealed highrises, all hooked up with an environmentally devastating infrastructure of roads, highways, storm and sanitary sewers, power lines, and the rest.[11] The pattern of these templates has become the pattern of our everyday experience, insinuating itself into our own awareness of place and nature.

City planners, engineers, and other design professionals have gotten trapped in standardized solutions that require enormous expenditures of energy and resources to implement. These standard templates, available as off-the-shelf recipes, are unconsciously adopted and replicated on a vast scale. The result might be called *dumb design:* design that fails to consider the health of human communities or of ecosystems, let alone the prerequisites of creating an actual place.

Dumb design is wasteful of energy and resources. It is polluting, extravagant, and profoundly dangerous. Unfortunately, we are surrounded by it. We have let dumb design come to dominate the scene because we lacked the words and awareness to fight it. We have been late to acknowledge that the environmental crisis is also a crisis of design, and slow to generate forms of knowledge and policies that might favor more sensible kinds of design. We have created sterile places because we have not honored the small, constant acts of compassion required to care for the living world.

On the other hand, if we build a rich enough set of ecological concerns into the very epistemology of design, we may create a coherent response to the environmental crisis. In Germany, manufacturers are now required by law to either take back and recycle old packaging or pay a steep tax. This has transformed the epistemology of the German packaging industry. Now new questions occur in the packaging design process: How can durability and reuse be designed into the packaging? How can easy disassembly of packaging components to facilitate recycling be designed into the packaging? These questions have triggered extraordinary innovations in reusable or recyclable packaging with corresponding environmental benefits including decreased waste and use of virgin materials. In contrast, dumb design doesn't ask the right questions. It blindly optimizes with respect to cost or convenience while neglecting environmental considerations.

If the assumptions underlying our agriculture include maximum productivity and minimum workers per acre, monoculture, cheap fuel and fertilizer, infinite availability of soil, and the irrelevance of negative health effects from pesticides, we will use our land much as we do in the American Midwest. These assumptions were taken to their logical extreme in a 1970 *National Geographic* article, "The Revolution in American Agriculture," which included a two-page illustration of life on the farm in the early twenty-first century. The caption says it all: "Grainfields stretch like fairways and cattle pens resemble high-rise apartments. . . . Attached to a modernistic farmhouse, a bubble-topped control tower hums with a computer, weather reports, and a farm-price ticker tape . . . a jet-powered helicopter sprays insecticides. . . . Across a service road, conical mills blend feed for beef cattle, fattening in multilevel pens that conserve ground space. Tubes carry the feed to be mechanically distributed."[12] The U.S. Department of Agriculture produced this particular projection without any apparent ironic intent.

Changing the assumptions underlying agriculture—the epistemology of farming—clearly produces a different result. Small organic farms are beginning to flourish again by minimizing inputs of fuel and fertilizer; providing healthy working conditions; diversifying crops to give protection against weeds, pests, and diseases; and conserving soil. If we view the growing of food as a design problem embedded in a wider cultural and ecological context, it begins to echo other design problems. Many of the same considerations that inform ecologically sound agriculture also inform the design of sound packaging systems, the design of sane energy systems, or the design of environmentally sensitive buildings.

The case of architecture is typical. For most of this century, architectural design has been informed by the metaphor of the machine. At best, nature is seen as a picturesque backdrop to the dominant form, the piece of architecture itself, representing an expression of unfettered creative will. Mies Van Der Rohe's Farnsworth House just outside of Chicago, which has influenced generations of modernist architects, is an example of a pristine technological statement that draws its power from appearing to be abstractly placed in its Midwest riparian setting. The landscape seems undisturbed. The floor and roof plans hover above the floodplain, raised on precise steel columns painted white. The trees on the riverbank are reflected in the ceiling-to-floor glass. The house is an object that draws its power from its spartan machinelike quality juxtaposed against its verdant natural setting.

Much of what architects have designed since the invention of the camera and of architectural magazines is heavily influenced by images, by surface rather than depth. Architects sometimes boast of the buildings they have designed without ever visiting the site. The exhibit halls in our leading architecture schools are filled with student projects consisting of models of buildings that seem to respond only to a cryptic logic of their own. Architecture is sometimes taught and envisioned as though sites were interchangeable background slides projected behind the manmade object.

The Farnsworth House is an example of the best that the metaphor of the machine has produced in relation to nature. At its worst, the metaphor of the machine allows us to see nature as a passive and malleable resource, ready to be refashioned into useful products. We have only to look at the millions of acres of wetlands, hills, forests, and farmlands that are converted to urban and suburban uses every year in order to comprehend the dominant attitude toward natural landscapes and places.

Before the energy crises of the 1970s, architects went about their work without possessing any vocabulary for the environmental impacts intrinsic to buildings. Such impacts were invisible because the prevailing architectural epistemology considered buildings as abstract, static forms with no internal living processes and no significant exchanges with the larger environment. There was no way to talk about the energy required to manufacture and transport building materials or about the building's climate responsiveness. As a result, these factors played no role in the design process, and the underlying epistemology was manifested in grotesquely inefficient buildings.

Unfortunately, at most universities it is *still* possible to earn a master's degree in architecture without knowing how the sun moves through the sky, without being aware of energy or resource use in buildings, without constructing anything, and without taking a course in environmental science. This tells us what counts for valid knowledge in the architectural profession and helps explain why 40 percent of the energy consumption in the United States can be traced to building construction, materials, and maintenance.

Despite these continuing trends, recent efforts by the American Institute of Architects (AIA) and many committed individual architects are moving toward a more environmentally nuanced architectural epistemology. For example, in the Croxton Collaborative's recent renovation of the Audubon building in New York City, a rich set of environmental criteria guided the design process.[13] Attempts were made to salvage as many building materials as possible during the construction process, to design the renovated building itself to be easily recyclable, to maximize daylighting and passive solar heating, to use nontoxic paints and finishes, and to facilitate the recycling of office materials during the entire life of the building. These criteria, used flexibly and creatively, brought in an environmentally sound building at just a few percent over the cost of a standard renovation.

If we are to take sustainability seriously, we must admit to ourselves that the emperor has no clothes: conventional design is failing because its epistemology is flawed. Gas courses into the tank, the dials spin 'round on the pump—this much is visible and immediate. What is less visible is the climate change being induced by the rapid and widescale use of fossil fuels. In the same way, farming practices that do not account for the health of water or soil, industrial processes that produce vast quantities of known carcinogens, and buildings that deplete resources and off-gas formaldehyde can be designed only within environmentally impoverished epistemologies.

In *Steps to an Ecology of Mind,* the anthropologist Gregory Bateson pursued a similar theme: "You decide that you want to get rid of the by-products of human life and that Lake Erie will be a good place to put them. You forget that the eco-mental system called Lake Erie is a part of your wider eco-mental system—and that if Lake Erie is driven insane, its insanity is incorporated in the larger system of your thought and experience."[14] Some even speak of the ecological unconscious, the deep, unacknowledged pain we feel for the ecological destruction all around us.[15]

The Farallones Institute Rural Center in Occidental, California, was once issued a citation for using improperly pasteurized milk from an "unauthorized source": its cow! In the same vein, the California Department of Transportation calls pedestrians "non-motorized units." Those of us who belong to industrial societies have come to utterly depend on far-flung sources for the basics of life. We have learned not to ask too many questions about how these basics are provided to us. We have individually and collectively denied the interdependence of nature and culture. The tragedy is that dumb design has provided so little of enduring value at such a great environmental and social cost. The industrialized world, with its science, technology, and borrowed affluence, has developed by denying wholeness within the art of living.

We need to ask questions, to intervene, to render visible what has so long been hidden from public discussion: that sustainability, or its lack, is inseparable from the particular characteristics of the objects, buildings, and landscapes we design. What is an appropriate level of density for a town? How can land-use patterns be made more conducive to the needs of wildlife? The details of design give a new tool for understanding and implementing sustainability.

We can learn a great deal by moving beyond abstract statements of policy toward the particulars of design. It is here, at the level of actual farms, buildings, or manufacturing processes, that relationships of culture and nature are thrown in sharp relief. It is here that the contours of a sustainable world beome definable.

## NOTES

1. The literature on the global environmental crisis is truly bewildering. Marxists blame capitalists, and capitalists blame market inefficiencies. Some, like Paul Ehrlich, see the population explosion as a driving force, while others view it as an effect of political and economic inequities. Scientists blame a lack of scientific knowledge among decision makers; others see science as the problem. In this book, we limit ourselves to the connection between design and sustainability.

2. David W. Orr, *Ecological Literacy: Education and the Transition to a Postmodern World* (Albany: State Univ. of New York Press, 1992), 24.

3. Ibid.

4. World Commission on Environment and Development, *Our Common Future* (New York: Oxford Univ. Press, 1987), 43.

5. Ibid., 89.

6. Wolfgang Sachs, "Global Ecology and the Shadow of 'Development,'" in *Global Ecology: A New Arena of Political Conflict,* ed. Wolfgang Sachs (London: Zed Books, 1993), 19.

7. Gustavo Esteva and Madhu Suri Prakash, "Grassroots Resistance to Sustainable Development: Lessons from the Banks of the Narmada," *The Ecologist* 22, no. 2 (March–April 1992): 45–51.

8. Orr, *Ecological Literacy,* 29–38.

9. Sean Wellesley-Miller, "Towards a Symbiotic Architecture," in *Earth's Answer: Explorations of Planetary Culture at the Lindisfarne Conferences,* ed. Michael Katz, William P. Marsh, and Gail Gordon Thompson (New York: Harper & Row, 1977), 82–3.

10. Wendell Berry, *The Gift of Good Land: Further Essays Cultural and Agricultural* (San Francisco: North Point Press, 1981), 135.

11. For more details on this kind of nowhere design, see Joel Garreau, *Edge City: Life on the New Frontier* (New York: Doubleday, 1991), and James Kunstler, *The Geography of Nowhere: The Rise and Decline of America's Man-Made Landscape* (New York: Simon & Schuster, 1993).

12. Jules Billard, "The Revolution in American Agriculture," *National Geographic* 137, no. 2 (February 1970): 184–5.

13. See National Audubon Society and Croxton Collaborative, Architects,

*Audubon House: Building the Environmentally Responsible, Energy-Efficient Office* (New York: John Wiley & Sons), 1994.

14. Gregory Bateson, *Steps to an Ecology of Mind* (New York: Ballantine Books, 1972), 484.

15. See, especially, Theodore Roszak, *The Voice of the Earth* (New York: Simon & Schuster), 1992.

# AN INTRODUCTION
# TO ECOLOGICAL
# DESIGN

OVERVIEW

We live in two interpenetrating worlds. The first is the living world, which has been forged in an evolutionary crucible over a period of four billion years. The second is the world of roads and cities, farms and artifacts, that people have been designing for themselves over the last few millennia. The condition that threatens both worlds—unsustainability—results from a lack of integration between them.

Now imagine the natural world and the humanly designed world bound together in intersecting layers, the warp and woof that make up the fabric of our lives. Instead of a simple fabric of two layers, it is made up of dozens of layers with vastly different characteristics. How these layers are woven together determines whether the result will be a coherent fabric or a dysfunctional tangle.

We need to acquire the skills to effectively interweave human and natural design. The designed mess we have made of our neighborhoods, cities, and ecosystems owes much to the lack of a coherent philosophy, vision, and practice of design that is grounded in a rich understanding of ecology. Unfortunately, the guiding metaphors of those who shape the built environment still reflect a nineteenth-century epistemology. Until our everyday activities preserve ecological integrity *by design*, their cumulative impact will continue to be devastating.

Thinking ecologically about design is a way of strengthening the weave that links nature and culture. Just as architecture has traditionally concerned itself with problems of structure, form, and aesthetics, or as engineering has with safety and efficiency, we need to consciously cultivate an ecologically sound form of design that is consonant with the long-term survival of all species. We define *ecological design* as "any form of design that minimizes environmentally destructive impacts by integrating itself with living processes." This integration implies that the design respects species diversity, minimizes resource depletion, preserves nutrient and water cycles, maintains habitat quality, and attends to all the other preconditions of human and ecosystem health.

Ecological design explicitly addresses the design dimension of the environmental crisis. It is not a style. It is a form of engagement and partnership with nature that is not bound to a particular design profession. Its scope is rich enough to embrace the work of architects rethinking their choices of building materials, the Army Corps of Engineers reformulating its flood-control strategy, and industrial designers curtailing their use of toxic compounds. Ecological design provides a coherent framework for redesigning our landscapes, buildings, cities, and systems of energy, water, food, manufacturing, and waste.

Ecological design is simply the effective *adaptation to* and *integration with* nature's processes. It proceeds from considerations of health and wholeness, and tests its solutions with a careful accounting of their *full* environmental impacts. It compels us to ask new questions of each design: Does it enhance and heal the living world, or does it diminish it? Does it preserve relevant ecological structure and process, or does it degrade it?

We are just beginning to make a transition from conventional forms of design, with the destructive environmental impacts they entail, to ecologically sound forms of design. There are now sewage treatment plants that use constructed marshes to simultaneously purify water, reclaim nutrients, and provide habitat. There are agricultural systems that mimic natural ecosystems and merge with their surrounding landscapes. There are new kinds of industrial systems in which the waste streams from one process are *designed* to be useful inputs to the next, thus minimizing pollution. There are new kinds of nontoxic paints, glues, and finishes. Such examples are now rapidly multiplying, and they play an important role in the chapters that follow.

We have already made dramatic progress in many areas by substituting design intelligence for the extravagant use of energy and materials. Computing power that fifty years ago would fill a house full of vacuum tubes and wires can now be held in the palm of your hand. The old steelmills whose blast furnaces, slag heaps, and towering smokestacks dominated the industrial landscape have been replaced with efficient scaled-down facilities and processes. Drafty, polluting fireplaces have been replaced with compact, highly efficient ones that burn pelletized wood wastes. Many products and processes have been miniaturized, with the flow of energy and materials required to make and operate them often dramatically reduced.

These examples show that when we think differently about design, new solutions are often quick to emerge. By explicitly taking ecology as the basis of design, we can vastly diminish the environmental impacts of everything we make and build.[1] While we've often done well in applying design intelligence to narrowly circumscribed problems, we now need to integrate ecologically sound technologies, planning methods, and policies across scales and professional boundaries.

The nutrients, energy, and information essential to life flow smoothly across scales ranging from microorganisms to continents; in contrast, design has become fragmented into dozens of separate technical disciplines, each with its own specialized language and tools. As the inventor Buckminster Fuller once noted, "Nature did not call a department heads' meeting when I threw a green apple into the pond, with the department heads having to make a decision about how to handle this biological encounter with chemistry's water and the unauthorized use of the physics department's waves."[2] No amount of regulation, intervention, or standalone brilliance will bring us a healthier world until we begin to deliberately join design decisions into coherent patterns that are congruent with nature's own.

In a sense, evolution is nature's ongoing design process. The wonderful thing about this process is that it is happening continuously throughout the entire biosphere. A typical organism has undergone at least a million years of intensive research and development, and none of our own designs can match that standard. Evolution has endowed individual organisms with a wide range of abilities, from harvesting sunshine to perceiving the world. Further, it has enabled communities of organisms to collectively recycle nutrients, regulate water cycles, and maintain both structure and diversity. Evolution has patiently worked on the living world to create a nested series of coherent levels, from organism to planet, each manifesting its own design integrities.

A few years ago, two Norwegian researchers set out to determine the bacterial diversity of a pinch of beech-forest soil and a pinch of shallow coastal sediment. They found well over four thousand species in each sample, which more than equaled the number listed in the standard catalogue of bacterial diversity. Even more remarkably, the species present in the two samples were almost completely distinct.[3] This extraordinary diversity pervades the Earth's manifold habitats, from deep-sea volcanic vents to mangrove swamps, from Arctic tundra to redwood forests. It is a diversity predicated on precise adaptation to underlying conditions. Within this diversity, within a hawk's wings or a nitrogen-fixing bacterium's enzymes, lies a rich kind of design competence. In nature, there is a careful choreography of function and form bridging many scales. It is this dance that provides the wider context for our own designs. In the attempt to minimize environmental impacts, we are inevitably drawn to nature's own design strategies.

These strategies form a rich resource for design guidance and inspiration. Contemplating the patterns that sustain life, we are given crucial design clues. We learn that spider plants are particularly good at removing pollutants from the air and might serve as an effective component of a living system for purifying the confined air of office buildings. We discover that wetlands can remove vast quantities of nutrients, detoxify compounds, and neutralize pathogens, and therefore can play a role in an ecological wastewater treatment system. The sum of these simple lessons from nature's own exquisite design catalog is nothing less than a blueprint for our own survival.

Suppose we represent our working "natural capital"—forests, lakes, wetlands, salmon, and so on—with a stack of coins. This natural capital provides renewable interest in the form of sustainable fish and timber yields, crops, and clean air, water, and soil. At present, we are simply spending this capital, drawing it down to dangerously low levels, decreasing the ability of remaining ecosystems to assimilate ever-increasing quantities of waste. Such an approach cannot help but deplete natural capital.

Ecological design offers three critical strategies for addressing this loss: conservation, regeneration, and stewardship. Conservation slows the rate at which things are getting worse by allowing scarce resources to be stretched further. Typical conservation measures include recycling materials, building denser communities to preserve agricultural land, adding insulation, and designing fuel-efficient cars. Unfortunately, conservation implicitly assumes that damage must be done and that the only recourse is to somehow minimize this damage. Conservation alone cannot lead to sustainability since it still implies an annual natural-resource deficit.

In the years before his death, Robert Rodale, editor of Rodale Press, was very concerned with what he termed *regeneration*. In a literal sense, regeneration is the repair and renewal of living tissue. Ecological design works to regenerate a world deeply wounded by environmentally insensitive design. This may involve restoring an eroded stream to biological productivity, re-creating habitat, or renewing soil. Regeneration is an expansion of natural capital through the active restoration of degraded ecosystems and communities. It is a form of healing and renewal that embodies the richest possibilities of culture to harmonize with nature. Regeneration not only preserves and protects: It restores a lost plenitude.

Stewardship is a particular quality of care in our relations with other living creatures and with the landscape. It is a process of steady commitment informed by constant feedback—for example, the gully is eroding, or Joe's doing poorly in math. It requires the careful maintenance and continual reinvestment that a good gardener might practice through weeding, watering, watching for pests, enriching the soil with compost, or adding new varieties. Stewardship maintains natural capital by spending frugally and investing wisely.

Ecological design embraces conservation, regeneration, and stewardship alike. If conservation involves spending natural capital more slowly, and regeneration is the expansion of natural capital, then stewardship is the wisdom to live on renewable interest rather than eating into natural capital. Conservation is already well established in the engineering and resource-management professions, but regeneration is just beginning to be explored by restoration ecologists, organic farmers, and others. Stewardship is a quality that all of us already have to some degree. Together, conservation, regeneration, and stewardship remind us of both the technical and personal dimensions of sustainability. They open up new kinds of creative endeavor even as they reaffirm the need for limits.

Careful ecological design permits such a great reduction in energy and material flows that human communities can once again be deeply integrated into their surrounding ecological communities. By carefully tailoring the scale and composition of wastes to the ability of ecosystems to assimilate them, we may begin to re-create a symbiotic relationship between nature and culture. By letting nature do the work, we allow ecosystems to flourish even as they purify and reclaim wastes, ameliorate the climate, provide food, or control flooding. It is clear that "the world is a vast repository of unknown biological strategies that could have immense relevance should we develop a science of integrating the stories embedded in nature into the systems we design to sustain us." [4] Ecological design begins to integrate these biological strategies by gently improvising upon life's own chemical vocabulary, geometry, flows, and patterns of community.

For example, if we wish to buttress a badly eroding hill, a conventional design might call for a concrete retaining wall many inches thick to hold the earth in place. Such a wall makes ostentatious use of matter and energy and does little to heal the land. In looking for an ecological design solution, we seek natural processes that perform this same work of holding the earth in place. We are led to trees, and a useful solution in practice has been to seed the hill with hundreds of willow branches. Within months the branches sprout, providing effective soil stabilization. The willow's articulated roots are far more adapted to keeping the soil in place than concrete, which bears only a superficial relationship to the soil. [5]

Ecological design occurs in the context of specific places. It grows out of place the way the oak grows from an acorn. It responds to the particularities of place: the soils, vegetation, animals, climate, topography, water flows, and people lending it coherence. It seeks locally adapted solutions that can replace matter, energy, and waste with design intelligence. Such an approach matches biological diversity with cultural diversity rather than compromising both the way conventional solutions do.

To design with this kind of care, we need to rigorously assess a design's set of environmental impacts. To take a simple example, consider just a few of the impacts of a typical house. Carbon dioxide emissions from the manufacture of the cement in its foundation contribute to global warming. The production of the electricity used to heat the house may contribute to acid rain in the region. Altered topography and drainage on-site may cause erosion, impacting the immediate watershed. The house might displace existing wildlife habitat. Inside the house, the health of the occupants may be compromised by emissions from the various glues, resins, and finishes used during construction. The lumber may have hastened the destruction of distant ancient forests. We are left with a somewhat disheartening picture of the wider ecological costs of a single building.

Ecological design converts these impacts from invisible side effects into explicitly incorporated design constraints. If ordinary cement's contribution to global warming renders its large-scale use undesirable, this imposes a critical design constraint. Perhaps the house can be sited in a way that minimizes cement use, or alternative, less-destructive cements can be used. If heating the house requires excessive quantities of electricity or natural gas, it may be possible to use passive solar heating through careful orientation of the building and the proper choice of building materials. In a similar way, each of the impacts can be turned into a stimulus for ecological design innovation.

Ecological design brings natural flows to the foreground. It celebrates the flow of water on the landscape, the rushing wind, the fertility of the earth, the plurality of species, and the rhythms of the sun, moon, and tides. It renders the invisible visible, allowing us to speak of it and carry it in our lives. It brings us back home. As the elements of our survival—the provenance of our food and energy, the veins of our watershed, the contours of our mountains—become vivid and present once again, they ground us in our place. We are given news of our region and the comings and goings of our fellow species. Ultimately, ecological design deepens our sense of place, our knowledge of both its true abundance and its unsuspected fragility.

Ecological design is a way of integrating human purpose with nature's own flows, cycles, and patterns. It begins with the richest possible understanding of the ecological context of a given design problem and develops solutions that are consistent with the cultural context. Such design cannot be the work of experts only. It is ultimately the work of a sustainable culture, one skilled in reweaving the multiple layers of natural and human design. Ecological designers are facilitators and catalysts in the cultural processes underlying sustainability.

We are beginning to get the pieces right, from highly efficient appliances to organic farms. However, until the pieces constitute the *texture* of everyday life, they will remain insufficient. This book is about the design wherewithal necessary to create a sustainable world. It provides a new way of seeing and thinking about design. It suggests a new set of questions and themes to order the design process. It proposes a form of design that is able to translate the vision of sustainability into the everyday objects, buildings, and landscapes around us. It embraces the best of the new ecological technologies but also inquires into the cultural foundations of sustainability. In short, it is an exploration of practical harmonies between nature and culture.

Table 1 compares conventional and ecological design in relation to a number of relevant issues.

### HISTORY AND BACKGROUND

Ecological design is not a new idea. By necessity, it has been brought to a high level of excellence by many different cultures faced with widely varying conditions. The Yanomamö, living with a refined knowledge of the Amazon rainforest, deliberately propagate hundreds of plant species, thereby enhancing biological diversity. Balinese aquaculture and rice terracing maintain soil fertility and pure water while feeding large numbers of people. Australian aborigines use stories and rituals to preserve an exquisitely detailed ecological map of their lands. The design rules embedded in each of these cultures have enabled them to persist for millennia.

TABLE I. Characteristics of Conventional and Ecological Design

| Issue | Conventional Design | Ecological Design |
|---|---|---|
| Energy source | Usually nonrenewable and destructive, relying on fossil fuels or nuclear power; the design consumes natural capital | Whenever feasible, renewable: solar, wind, small-scale hydro, or biomass; the design lives off solar income |
| Materials use | High-quality materials are used clumsily, and resulting toxic and low-quality materials are discarded in soil, air, and water | Restorative materials cycles in which waste for one process becomes food for the next; designed-in reuse, recycling, flexibility, ease of repair, and durability |
| Pollution | Copious and endemic | Minimized; scale and composition of wastes conform to the ability of ecosystems to absorb them |
| Toxic substances | Common and destructive, ranging from pesticides to paints | Used extremely sparingly in very special circumstances |
| Ecological accounting | Limited to compliance with mandatory requirements like environmental-impact reports | Sophisticated and built in; covers a wide range of ecological impacts over the entire life-cycle of the project, from extraction of materials to final recycling of components |
| Ecology and economics | Perceived as in opposition; short-run view | Perceived as compatible; long-run view |
| Design criteria | Economics, custom, and convenience | Human and ecosystem health, ecological economics |
| Sensitivity to ecological context | Standard templates are replicated all over the planet with little regard to culture or place; skyscrapers look the same from New York to Cairo | Responds to bioregion: the design is integrated with local soils, vegetation, materials, culture, climate, topography; the solutions grow from place |

| Issue | Conventional Design | Ecological Design |
|---|---|---|
| Sensitivity to cultural context | Tends to build a homogeneous global culture; destroys local commons | Respects and nurtures traditional knowledge of place and local materials and technologies; fosters commons |
| Biological, cultural, and economic diversity | Employs standardized designs with high energy and materials throughput, thereby eroding biological, cultural, and economic diversity | Maintains biodiversity and the locally adapted cultures and economies that support it |
| Knowledge base | Narrow disciplinary focus | Integrates multiple design disciplines and wide range of sciences; comprehensive |
| Spatial scales | Tends to work at one scale at a time | Integrates design across multiple scales, reflecting the influence of larger scales on smaller scales and smaller on larger |
| Whole systems | Divides systems along boundaries that do not reflect the underlying natural processes | Works with whole systems; produces designs that provide the greatest possible degree of internal integrity and coherence |
| Role of nature | Design must be imposed on nature to provide control and predictability and meet narrowly defined human needs | Includes nature as a partner: whenever possible, substitutes nature's own design intelligence for a heavy reliance on materials and energy |
| Underlying metaphors | Machine, product, part | Cell, organism, ecosystem |
| Level of participation | Reliance on jargon and experts who are unwilling to communicate with public limits community involvement in critical design decisions | A commitment to clear discussion and debate; everyone is empowered to join the design process |

(*table continues*)

TABLE I. (*continued*)

| Issue | Conventional Design | Ecological Design |
|---|---|---|
| Types of learning | Nature and technology are hidden; the design does not teach us over time | Nature and technology are made visible; the design draws us closer to the systems that ultimately sustain us |
| Response to sustainability crisis | Views culture and nature as inimical, tries to slow the rate at which things are getting worse by implementing mild conservation efforts without questioning underlying assumptions | Views culture and nature as potentially symbiotic; moves beyond triage to a search for practices that actively regenerate human and ecosystem health |

Even during the most uncritical growth eras of the industrialized nations, there have been strong movements for ecologically sound town planning, healthy building, organic agriculture, appropriate technology, renewable energy, and interdisciplinary approaches to design. William Morris's Arts and Crafts Movement, Rudolph Steiner's biodynamic agriculture, Ebenezer Howard's garden cities, Patrick Geddes's and Lewis Mumford's regional planning, and Frank Lloyd Wright's organic architecture—each celebrated design at a human scale firmly situated in a wider ecological context. Buckminster Fuller, in an enormously productive five decades of work, tested the limits of ephemeralization—decreasing the use of materials and energy—while designing Dymaxion houses that could process their own wastes and be recycled at the end of their useful lives.

By the 1960s, various streams of stubborn ethical and aesthetic opposition to unfettered industrialization coalesced into the first modern generation of ecological design. Designer Sean Wellesley-Miller and physicist Day Chahroudi designed building "skins" based on biological metaphors and principles but using newly available materials. John and

Nancy Todd and their associates at the New Alchemy Institute designed solar Arks that grew their own food, provided their own energy, and recycled their own wastes.[6] Other experimental houses and habitats were built all over the world, including the Ouroboros House in Minneapolis, the Autonomous House at Cambridge University, and the Farallones Institute's Integral Urban House in Berkeley, California. While different in form and purpose, all of these projects shared a similar vision: Biology and ecology are the key sciences in rethinking the design of habitat. Within these projects, the metaphor of a living organism or ecosystem replaced Le Corbusier's old image of a dwelling as a "machine for living."

The house, the habitat we are most familiar with, seemed to be a good place to start this first generation of ecological design. The rural or village homestead was once the center of a largely self-sufficient system that produced a family's livelihood, its food and fiber, and its tools and toys. Over a period of several hundred years, this homestead has become an anonymous mass-produced dwelling unit, its inhabitants members of a faceless consumershed, the house itself totally dependent on outside resources to sustain its inhabitants. Rethinking home metabolism became the mission of the first generation of ecological design.

The Integral Urban House, conceived by biologists Bill and Helga Olkowski and sponsored by the Farallones Institute, started in 1973 in a ramshackle Victorian house in Berkeley, California.[7] The oil embargo had made many people aware for the first time of their almost total dependence on an oil economy. Designers were challenged to work with the sun, turning this house from a consumer of oil for heating, cooling, electricity, and food into a producer of thermal energy, food, and electricity.

The Integral Urban House was intended to restore its inhabitants to a measure of control over the basics of their life support, reduce the outflow of money to pay for resources and services that the home and local environment could provide, and encourage interaction with local ecosystems. The idea was to integrate energy and food production and waste and water recycling directly into the home design. The Integral Urban House featured composting toilets, an aquaculture pond, organic gardens, and advanced recycling. The guiding vision was a new synthesis of architecture and biology.

During these years of creative ferment, important theoretical advances were also made. In *Design with Nature,* Ian McHarg looked at the natural functioning of landscapes and proposed that intelligent land-use planning be based on "what a landscape wants to be." In *Small Is Beautiful,* Fritz Schumacher, drawing heavily on the ideas of Gandhi, persuasively argued that small-scale systems made economic sense, thus launching the appropriate-technology movement. Amory Lovins provided a coherent solar alternative to nuclear energy in *Soft Energy Paths.* John and Nancy Todd provided nine key precepts for "biological design" in *Bioshelters, Ocean Arks, City Farming: Ecology as the Basis of Design,* recently republished as *From Eco-Cities to Living Machines: Principles of Ecological Design.* Christopher Alexander and colleagues presented a powerful new theory of design with important ecological ramifications in *A Pattern Language* and *The Timeless Way of Building.*

In the 1980s, the environmental movement grew into a broad-based sustainability movement. Great technical advances were made in solar and wind energy. Lovins's Rocky Mountain Institute helped transform energy policy in many nations. Bill Mollison's "permaculture" approach to organic agriculture and healthy building gained a worldwide following from its modest start in Tasmania. Fundamental research on sustainable agriculture was performed at the University of California, Santa Cruz, and the Land Institute in Salina, Kansas. Work in landscape ecology and conservation biology provided a new set of tools for preserving biodiversity that have been effectively used by Project Wild. Peter Calthorpe, Andres Duany, and Elizabeth Plater-Zyberk created renewed interest in pedestrian-oriented town planning.

The 1990s have seen the emergence of the international ecocities movement, which is working to create healthier, more resource-efficient cities. Constructed ecosystems—wetlands and contained microcosms—are rapidly becoming an important alternative to conventional wastewater treatment systems. Industrial ecology and life-cycle analysis are already key tools for minimizing pollution. New approaches to ecological restoration and toxic decontamination show great promise. Recent attempts to integrate ecology and economics are also beginning to bear fruit, including Pliny Fisk's approach to bioregional design at the Center for Maximum Potential Building Systems in Austin, Texas. Artists like Andy Goldsworthy and Mierle Ukeles are creating works that demonstrate a deep commitment to ecological ideas.

The 1980s and 1990s also saw the publication of a handful of important theoretical works related to ecological design. John Tillman Lyle's *Design for Human Ecosystems: Landscape, Land Use, and Natural Resources* and more recent *Regenerative Design for Sustainable Development* provide careful and comprehensive treatments of ecological design strategies. Robert L. Thayer, Jr.'s, *Gray World, Green Heart: Technology, Nature, and the Sustainable Landscape* is a more philosophical work that raises important issues. Sim Van der Ryn and Peter Calthorpe's *Sustainable Communities: A New Design Synthesis for Cities, Suburbs, and Towns* treats ecological design at the town scale. Paul Hawken's *The Ecology of Commerce: A Declaration of Sustainability* makes important connections between ecological design and business.

The first generation of ecological design was based on small-scale experiments with living lightly in place. Many of the technologies and ideas of this generation, such as alternative building materials, renewable energy, organic foods, conservation, and recycling have been widely adopted in piecemeal fashion. We now stand at the threshold of a second generation of ecological design. This second generation is not an alternative to dominant technology and design; it is the best path for their necessary evolution.

The second generation of ecological design must effectively weave the insights of literally dozens of disciplines. It must create a viable ecological design craft within a genuine culture of sustainability rather than getting entangled in interdisciplinary disputes and turf wars. It is time to bring forth new ecologies of design that are rich with cultural and epistemological diversity.

### NOTES

1. "Ecology as the basis of design" is a wonderful phrase that was used in the subtitle of the pioneering book *Bioshelters, Ocean Arks, City Farming: Ecology as the Basis of Design* by Nancy Jack Todd and John Todd (San Francisco: Sierra Club Books, 1984). The book is now available in an updated edition called *From Eco-Cities to Living Machines: Principles of Ecological Design* (Berkeley: North Atlantic Books, 1994).

2. Buckminster Fuller, *Synergetics: Explorations in the Geometry of Thinking* (New York: Macmillan, 1975), 108.

3. Edward O. Wilson, *The Diversity of Life* (Cambridge: Harvard Univ. Press, 1992), 144.

4. Nancy Jack Todd and John Todd, *From Eco-Cities*, 175.

5. More details of such an approach are provided by Hugo Schiechtl in *Bioengineering for Land Reclamation and Conservation* (Edmonton: Univ. of Alberta Press, 1980).

6. The Ark is fully documented by Nancy Jack Todd and John Todd in *Tomorrow Is Our Permanent Address: The Search for an Ecological Science of Design as Embodied in the Bioshelter* (New York: Harper & Row, 1980).

7. The Integral Urban House is exhaustively described by Helga Olkowski et al. in *The Integral Urban House: Self-Reliant Living in the City* (San Francisco: Sierra Club Books, 1979).

# NATURE'S GEOMETRY

## SCALE LINKING

Consider a drop of rain. Hidden within it is an implicit history of places: water gathered from ancient fjords, alpine lakes, urban reservoirs, Antarctic ice, all running together in a single cycle, ever changing yet unitary. The flow of water in the biosphere links Australia to Greenland and Rocky Mountain springs to the Ganges. Other natural cycles bind us to the living world as they carry nutrients and trace minerals between earth, air, and water.

These cycles connect together phenomena at very different spatial scales (characteristic lengths). Jumping in scale a thousandfold at each step, we encounter a drop of water at a scale of one millimeter, a puddle at one meter, a lake at one kilometer, and the Antarctic ice at one thousand kilometers.

Nature's processes are inherently *scale linking,* for they intimately depend on the flow of energy and materials across scales. The waste oxygen from blue-green algae is absorbed by a blue whale, whose own waste carbon dioxide feeds an oak tree. Global cycles link organisms together in a highly effective recycling system crossing about seventeen tenfold jumps in scale, from a ten-billionth of a meter (the scale of photosynthesis) to ten thousand kilometers (the scale of the Earth itself).

In a turbulent brook, eddies and whorls of all sizes grow and recede, send out tendrils, absorb their neighbors, and are in turn absorbed. Water is caught up in microscopic whirlpools and escapes to a larger scale, only to recede again to the microscopic. Scale-linking systems "imply a holism in which everything influences, or potentially influences, everything else—because everything is in some sense constantly interacting with everything else."[1] Nature is infused with the dynamical interpenetration of the vast and minute, an endless dervish mixing. Matter and energy continually flow across scales, the small informing the large and the large informing the small.

We are predisposed to seeing processes at a single scale, refracted through a single discipline's language, metaphors, and tools. In practice, this kind of perception is insufficient to capture the underlying phenomena. Suppose we were to determine the characteristic scale of acid rain. Is it the scale of a coal-fired power plant, spewing forth nitrogen and sulfur oxides? Or is it the scale of an individual house, feeding from that power plant? Is it the scale of an unhealthy lake, whose fish are dying as the water grows increasingly acidic? One might argue that the scale is regional, embracing an entire network of power plants. Canadians, angered by the disastrous impacts of American coal plants on their own lakes and forests, believe the scale of acid rain is international. Then again, perhaps we have missed the point: Isn't the true scale of acid rain molecular, embedded in the intricate process chemistry of coal combustion?

It is clear that each of these possible scales of analysis has both some validity and some institutional support. Legions of experts study, respectively, pollution-control measures for power plants, energy-efficient homes, the ecology of lakes undergoing acidification, the atmospheric dynamics of pollution, the international legal implications of acid rain, and the chemistry of coal combustion. Acid rain involves the flow of various contaminants across many levels of scale. If we focus on a single scale, we miss the other scales, and hence miss opportunities to work across them in a unified way to address the problem.

The acid-rain example demonstrates that the ecological impacts of design activities cross scales and political jurisdictions. A house, a hydroelectric dam, and a wastewater system have impacts that are not neatly confined to a single scale. What we do at one scale has subtle impacts, both negative and positive, at many other scales. Scale linking reminds us of the wider environmental consequences of our designs.

Unless we work with nature's own finely tuned scale-linking systems, we endanger the stability of life on this planet. We have already increased atmospheric carbon dioxide by one-fourth since preindustrial times, with important implications for the global climate. Even in remote regions, background levels of lead have increased by up to one thousand times.[2] Our industry and agriculture already generate annual flows of heavy metals, sulfur, and other elements that are greater than their natural counterparts.

If we are to properly include ecological concerns within design, we must take seriously the challenge offered by scale linking. We need to discover ways to integrate our design processes across multiple levels of scale and make these processes compatible with natural cycles of water, energy, and materials.

In the 1920s, an eccentric Englishman named Lewis Richardson asked a deceptively simple question: What is the length of Britain's coastline? As he looked at more and more detailed maps, he noticed new features. An apparently straight stretch of coastline on a coarse map would resolve itself into a series of coves, bays, headlands, and peninsulas on a finer map. Over many levels of map scales, the rugged coastline looked qualitatively similar.

While a square has no hidden detail at a finer scale, the British coastline constantly reveals new features as it is magnified (figure 1). Remarkably, it is made of fragments that resemble the whole. It is woven from a new kind of geometry that connects scales. In this geometry, forms at one scale resemble forms at another scale because the processes shaping form are essentially identical across many scales. This geometry provides a

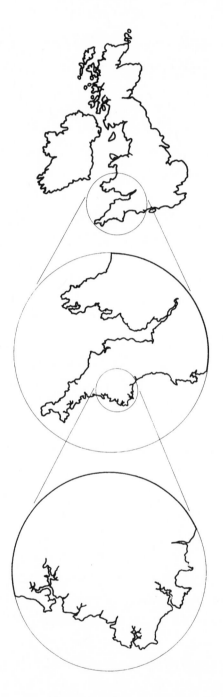

FIGURE I. *The coastline of Britain at successive scales of magnification*

useful metaphor for our own attempts to bridge design disciplines that span very different scales.

In recent years, mathematicians have begun studying geometrical forms sharing many properties of the British coastline. While these idealized forms are immune to the subtle chance factors that give a natural object its texture and irregularity, they provide simple and explicit models of geometries that link together multiple scales. Consider the construction of the *Koch curve*.

We start with a line segment.

Now we divide the segment into three parts.

Next, we build an equilateral triangle from the middle segment, erasing the base. We now have four segments, each with a length one-third of the original segment.

Now we apply the same process to each of the four new segments, adding a finer level of detail.

Applying the same process infinitely often, we obtain the Koch curve.

Each stage in the construction of the Koch curve adds subtler detail. The smallest existing level of scale forms a kind of skeleton for the articulation of form at the next, even smaller, level of scale. At each stage, the structure is organized by pushing the middle third of each segment out into a triangle. Since each fragment of the Koch curve is organized by the same processes that shape the whole curve, each fragment resembles the whole curve. In fact, it is easy to see that the Koch curve is made up of four exact 3:1 copies of itself.

Both the coastline of Britain and the Koch curve manifest a remarkable kind of symmetry that explicitly links multiple scales. The symmetry is a simple one: The whole form is built up from subforms that echo the whole. This symmetry has appropriately been dubbed *self-similarity*, and forms possessing it are termed *fractals*. Self-similarity is a direct consequence of identical processes shaping form across many scales.

Fractal geometry is the geometry of scale linking. It connects a remarkable range of scales, from twig to tree, from rivulet to watershed. Even our own bodies are infused with fractal forms: "The lymph system, the small intestine, the lungs, muscle tissue, connective tissue, the folding patterns on the surface of the brain, the calyx filters in the kidney, and the design of the bile ducts—all show [fractal] scaling. This fractal design vastly increases the surface area available for the distribution, collection, absorption, and excretion of a host of vital fluids and dangerous toxins that regularly course through the body."[3] The available *surface area* of the lungs or brain increases when viewed at finer and finer scales, just as the *length* of the British coastline does. Since the chemical interactions critical for healthy biological functioning proceed more efficiently when a greater surface area is available, this evolved geometry is appropriate for its task. Convoluted fractal forms are valuable precisely because—unlike spheres—they have extremely *high* surface-to-volume ratios. In contrast with the standard forms of Euclidean geometry, fractal forms facilitate the flow of energy and materials across multiple scales.

In nature, geometries reflect and enhance underlying processes. In a paper on the role of biological surfaces, the visionary biologist Paul Mankiewicz discusses the ability of the fractal root systems of plants to purify water.[4] In conventional wastewater treatment systems, bacteria flow along with the water to be treated. They absorb substances in their immediate vicinity through relatively inefficient diffusion processes. In contrast, ecological wastewater treatment systems facilitate rich chemical exchanges on the surfaces of the roots (figure 2). The roots actively order the flow of chemical energy, facilitating the work of the microorganisms that inhabit them. Preliminary research indicates that the vast surface area provided by the root systems permits nutrient filtering to be performed extremely efficiently.

Nature's geometry is an important organizing principle for ecological design. It determines the context for design, whether at the scale of a root system or an entire watershed. Over a century ago, Major John Wesley Powell, head of the U.S. Geological Survey, explicitly recognized this organizing principle in his suggestion to settle the arid West in a way that matched land allocations to the availability of water. Speaking to the Montana Statehood Convention in Helena on August 9, 1889, "he proposed to organize the new state of Montana into counties whose boundaries would be established by the divisions between hydrographic basins rather than by arbitrary political lines drawn on the map. Such basins, already being plotted out in Montana as in other parts of the west by his survey crews, were natural geographical and topographical unities; they might be given political and economic unity as well."[5] Powell foresaw the need to make water and homesteading laws reflect the fragile ecology of the West.

A project conducted in the San Francisco Bay Area provides a contemporary application of this principle. Geographer Josh Collins has been working with a mosquito abatement district to try to approximate the original fractal drainage fingers on a seventy-acre marsh on U.S. Navy land. After the marsh was disturbed by a road, it began to harbor some stagnant water, which served as a breeding ground for mosquitoes. In an attempt to eliminate this standing water, early mosquito abatement efforts focused on digging additional drainage ditches. These ditches—unaccompanied by an increase in tidal flux—were so effective that water no

*Bacteria flow with the water and absorb
nutrients through inefficient diffusion processes*

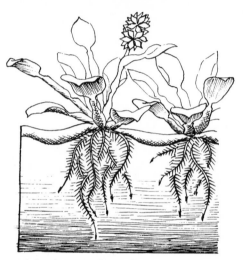

*A floating mat of water hyacinths showing
the fractal structure of the root system*

*The fractal roots grow into the flow, creating a vast surface area
for biological interactions and maximizing chemical gradients*

FIGURE 2. *Fractal roots and wastewater treatment*

longer entered the upper reaches of natural channels. Portions of the upper channels filled in, creating the very potholes the mosquito abatement efforts were trying to avoid. As Collins notes, "The ditches previously created for mosquito reduction are not alleviating the problem. In fact, the marshes with the most extensive ditch networks often generate the most mosquitoes. This is because the number, size, and arrangement of these ditches were not determined in relation to marsh geomorphology and tidal hydrology."[6] By augmenting total tidal flow, severing drainage ditches connecting distinct drainage basins, and adding new ditches, Collins and colleagues have been able to partially restore the original fit between the geometry of the marsh's drainage fingers and the character of the tidal flux. The new system is working well, and the marsh not only is mosquito-free but also is attracting shorebirds previously unknown at the site.

Geological processes operate in a self-similar way over a vast range of scales, producing a variety of fractal systems: coastlines, archipelagos, mountains, watershed drainages, fault lines, mineral deposits, and so on. Vegetation responds to these fractal landscape features, with each plant favoring a particular microclimate and set of soil conditions. Vegetation, in turn, is a major determinant of ecosystem structure and animal habitat. Fractal geological forms are ultimately reflected in fractal habitats.

Just as the earlier mosquito abatement efforts failed because they ignored the geometry of the marsh's drainage fingers, current political and planning boundaries do not reflect the underlying structures and flows of landscapes. It is as if blood cells moving from one part of the body to another had to obtain travel visas. Our watersheds are divided up among towns, counties, states, and countries. The strip of cleared vegetation marking the Canada–U.S. border is visible in satellite photos, an ecologically meaningless line on a landscape otherwise filled with subtle harmonies.

Twenty-five years ago, landscape architect and planner Ian McHarg proposed a system of constraint maps that were intended to help planners identify ecologically sensitive areas. His plea for a more responsive method of environmental planning remains just as valid today: "Where planning does occur, its single instrument is zoning and by this device political subdivisions are allocated densities irrespective of geology, physiography, hydrology, soils, vegetation, scenery, or historic beauty. The adoption of the ecological method would at least produce . . . a structure of open space wherein nature performed work for man, or wherein development was dangerous."[7] Over time, perhaps we will learn to discern the integrities and continuities, the match of geometry and flow, inherent in a region's geology, hydrology, soils, and vegetation.

Our ecological crises have resulted, in part, from a failure to match human flows of energy and materials to the limits of the landscape. The geometry of the landscape is manifested in the distribution of agricultural lands, minerals, wetlands, forests, and other primary resources. We have not followed this geometry. We have overstepped local limits and relied on far-flung ecological subsidies. A good example is provided by the vast water diversion projects that maintain life in desert towns like Los Angeles, Phoenix, and Las Vegas. While this refusal to acknowledge the limitations of place has many aspects, it is also a design issue. If we impose a Cartesian grid on a fractal landscape, settlements will be too large or small, flows will not be of a sensible scale, and we will compromise the ecological resources we depend on.

In contrast, by matching the flows on a landscape to its inherent geometry, we allow ecological patterns to work for us. We can use natural drainage instead of storm drains, wetlands instead of sewage treatment plants, and indigenous materials rather than imported ones. We can work toward a steady convergence of dwelling, design, and the geometry of place.

We are surrounded by a fractal landscape—clouds, mountains, river networks—and surely this has left us a fondness for the reconciliation and interweaving of multiple scales so characteristic of fractal geometry. This geometry teaches us a new kind of attentiveness, one that recognizes that

FIGURE 3. *Hokusai's Great Wave, illustrating*
*self-similar waves at many levels of scale*

"the landscape is the crucible in which living forms have evolved, and since the landscape crackles with fractals, the forms bred there are fractal as well."[8] This geometry reminds us that nature is constantly linking scales, bringing together the respiration of the blue whale and the photosynthesis of the oak in a single dance.

### CREATING A DESIGN DIALOGUE ACROSS SCALES

Our present level of design integration across scales resembles the profusion of U.S. railroads in the mid-nineteenth century, each with its own gauge of tracks. The courageous cross-continental traveler would frequently transfer from one train to another since the gauges were incompatible. Architects, urban planners, industrial designers—design professionals of all stripes—are clinging to their own gauges, their own scales of interest and expertise. Of course, each field *does* work at a different scale, and *does* incorporate certain specialized knowledge, but each must work within a common background of scale-linking processes that cross disciplinary boundaries. The challenge is to create a dialogue that links the insights of designers working at different levels of scale. Without a common gauge, a shared dialogue, we will continue to face the costs associated with rigidly segregated disciplines: mutual incomprehension and designs that work at cross-purposes.

In contrast, ecological design is not bound to a particular scale. It provides a way of uniting diverse design perspectives—and the different scales they represent—by testing them against strong ecological constraints. As we connect design across multiple scales, opportunities appear. For instance, we find that environmental planners can work not just for open space, but for critical wildlife corridors spanning biological reserves hundreds of kilometers apart. It is possible to design soaps that not only clean well but are biologically compatible with soils and streams. New glazing technologies, appropriate choices of building materials, and sensible solar siting can together eliminate the need for a conventional heating system. In each case, a wider design dialogue allows a deeper integration of design with nature.

The work of the Royal Commission on the Future of the Toronto Waterfront offers an excellent model for design across typically antagonistic professions and political jurisdictions. Since 1988, the commission has brought together diverse government agencies and citizens groups in an "ecosystem approach" to planning. According to the commission's final report, *Regeneration: Toronto's Waterfront and the Sustainable City*, this approach

- includes the whole system, not just parts of it

- recognizes the ecosystem's dynamic nature, presenting a moving picture rather than a still photograph of it
- uses a broad definition of environments—natural, physical, economic, social, and cultural
- encompasses both urban and rural activities
- is based on natural geographic units such as watersheds, rather than on political boundaries
- embraces all levels of activity—local, regional, national, and international[9]

The Toronto watershed is afflicted with many different stresses. A very incomplete list would include emissions from factories and sewage treatment plants, agricultural runoff, household dumping of toxins in storm drains, acid rain and smog from the highly urbanized region, channelized creeks, habitat fragmentation from development, and deforestation. The commission has responded by recognizing a kind of "green infrastructure":

What if we were to start with the demand for natural systems? How much land should be allocated to nature? How much to other kinds of open spaces? What ecological, aesthetic, urban design, and recreational functions can they fulfill?

This would lead to a different way of structuring urban form, using a fully linked, continuous "green infrastructure," based on natural systems, and recognizing open space—not as an absence of buildings but as a land use in its own right. . . . A green infrastructure may include natural habitat areas; land-forms such as bluffs, valleys, tablelands, beaches, and cliffs; aquifers and recharge areas; rural lands; heritage landscapes; parks, trails, and other open spaces; and archaeological sites.[10]

The notion of green infrastructure hints at a holistic approach to pollution, biodiversity, and watershed health, acknowledging that a watershed requires coordinated governance and interdisciplinary approaches. Moreover, the *Regeneration* report is surprisingly frank about the inadequacies of existing political and planning jurisdictions in alleviating environmental problems that routinely transcend their boundaries. It states that "in the past, the parochial pressures of bureaucracies and representative governments have almost compelled them to be unresponsive to cross-jurisdictional issues. When everyone is in charge, no one is in charge."[11] The commission's work is a promising attempt to create a meaningful dialogue among design disciplines.

The Natural Step Foundation in Sweden has taken on an even more ambitious project: creating a strong interdisciplinary scientific consensus on the root causes of the environmental crisis. The Natural Step has brought together scientists and professionals from dozens of fields in a search for shared understanding and vision. The results have been summarized in a beautiful, simply written booklet distributed to every household in Sweden. The Natural Step has deeply influenced policymakers, businesspeople, and ordinary citizens. Founder Dr. K.-H. Robèrt states the motivation for such a project:

> Up to now, much of the debate over the environment has had the character of monkey chatter amongst the withering leaves of a dying tree — the leaves representing specific, isolated problems. We are confronted with a mass of seemingly insoluble questions. In the very midst of all this chatter about leaves, very few of us have been paying attention to the environment's trunk and branches. They are deteriorating as a result of processes about which there is little or no controversy; and the thousands of individual problems that are the subject of so much debate are, in fact, manifestations of systemic errors that are undermining the foundations of society.[12]

Both the Toronto waterfront and Natural Step projects are dialogues that reflect the inherent scale linking of natural processes. They bridge the language, the attitudes, and the fears that have kept the various scientific and design disciplines apart. Ecological design is an invitation to a similar dialogue, for without it, we will continue to find only fragmented solutions that are just precursors to further problems. We will continue to destroy that which is whole. On the other hand, if we begin such a dialogue in good faith, we may begin to find designs nuanced enough to honor the diversity and complexity of life itself.

NOTES

1. John Briggs, *Fractals: The Patterns of Chaos: Discovering a New Aesthetic of Art, Science, and Nature* (New York: Simon & Schuster, 1992), 21.
2. John Harte et al., *Toxics A to Z: A Guide to Everyday Pollution Hazards* (Berkeley and Los Angeles: Univ. of California Press, 1991), 333.
3. Briggs, *Fractals,* 124.
4. These comments rely on a manuscript version of Paul Mankiewicz's paper "Biological Surfaces, Metabolic Capacitance, Growth, and Differentiation: A Theoretical Exploration of Thermodynamic, Economic, and Material Efficiencies in Fluid Purification Systems," a 1993 report from the Center for Restoration of Waters, Falmouth, Mass.
5. Wallace Stegner, *Beyond the Hundredth Meridian: John Wesley Powell and the Second Opening of the West* (New York: Penguin Books, 1992), 315.
6. Vicki L. Kramer, Joshua N. Collins, and Charles Beesley, "Reduction of Salt Marsh Mosquitoes by Enhancing Tidal Action," *Proceedings of California Mosquito Vector Control Association* (1992): 21.
7. Ian McHarg, *Design with Nature* (Garden City, N.Y.: Natural History Press, 1969), 161.
8. Briggs, *Fractals,* 36.
9. Royal Commission on the Future of the Toronto Waterfront, *Regeneration: Toronto's Waterfront and the Sustainable City: Final Report* (Toronto: Queen's Printer of Ontario, 1992), xxii.
10. Ibid., 78.
11. Ibid., xxii.
12. K.-H. Robèrt, "Non-Negotiable Facts as a Basis for Decision-Making," a working paper for the Natural Step Foundation, Amiralitetshuset, Sweden, 1–2.

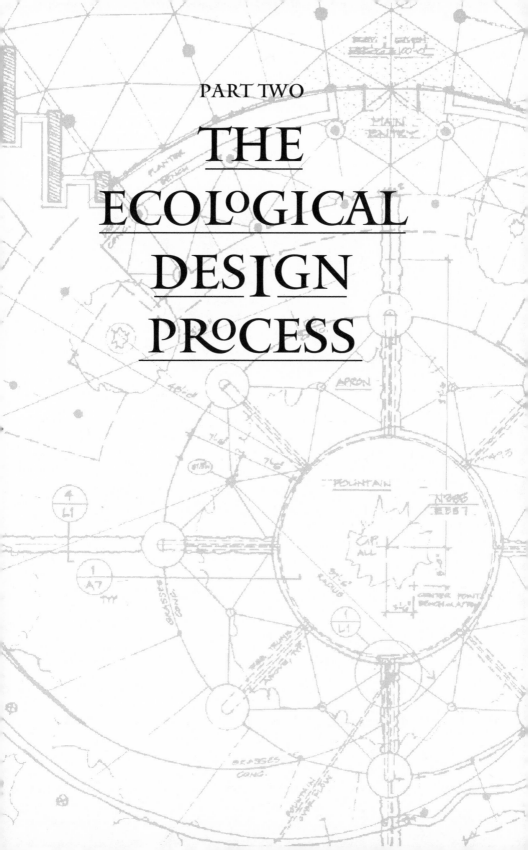

PART TWO

# THE ECOLOGICAL DESIGN PROCESS

# THE COMPOST
# PRIVY STORY

The chapters in Part Two introduce five broad principles of ecological design. The first principle grounds the design in the details of place. In the words of Wendell Berry, we need to ask, "What is here? What will nature permit us to do here? What will nature help us to do here?"[1] The second principle provides criteria for evaluating the ecological impacts of a given design. The third principle suggests that these impacts can be minimized by working in partnership with nature. The fourth principle implies that ecological design is the work not just of experts, but of entire communities. The fifth principle tells us that effective design transforms awareness by providing ongoing possibilities for learning and participation.

Taken together, these five principles help us to think about the integration of ecology and design. They can be readily illustrated by a seemingly humble example: the compost privy.[2]

In the late sixties and early seventies, many young people moved out of the cities into the rural backcountry to pursue their dream of living a more self-sufficient life closer to nature. Sim and his family were among those back-to-the-landers. As both a homesteader and an architect, he was often called upon to help these new rural dwellers attempting to build their own houses and to deal with wells, septic tanks, building codes, and local officialdom. Common problems—aside from lack of money—were water supply and the unavailability of suitable soils and slope to accommodate a leaching field to percolate wastewater. Many homesteaders worked hard to squeeze a meager amount of water out of seasonal springs, and they were not about to flush most of it down the toilet.

Sim's conversion to ecological awareness had occurred some years earlier, on an occasion when Walter, the graduate student who rented his downstairs apartment, came by for a cup of coffee. Sim threw the coffee grounds into the trashcan filled with food wrappers, cans, bottles, banana peels, steak bones, and leftover oatmeal. Walter wrinkled his nose, looked at Sim with benign disgust, and asked, "Don't you know how to compost?" They sorted through the trash, retrieved the organic wastes, and took them out to the yard, where they layered dead leaves, lawn clippings, and loose soil over them. Every few days Sim added more organic wastes, soil, and garden debris until the pile was about three feet high. Walter assisted and coached Sim those first months until graduation day, when they turned the pile. The bottom was now rich, crumbly, earthy-smelling compost.

Sim later helped redesign and rebuild an old house in Berkeley into a model urban ecological environment known as the Integral Urban House. The house had two composting bins, each about three feet by three feet. Properly managed, they worked like dynamite. The house also had a prototype "composting toilet"—the Clivus Multrum invented by an engineer for use in summer cabins built around glacial lakes in Sweden. The thin soil mantle and the cabins' close proximity to the lakes made it impossible to install standard septic tanks and leaching fields, which disperse wastewater into the soil through pipes perforated with drainage holes. The Clivus Multrum at the Integral Urban House was an ungainly contraption built of fiberglass, a tank about ten feet long by four feet wide installed in the basement. A large tube extended up from the basement to the underside of the toilet seat upstairs, and a smaller tube ran up to the kitchen to receive organic wastes. The tank's bottom was lined with peat moss. Waste materials fell in through the tubes at the top and, like a glacier, slowly decomposed their way toward an access panel at the front, where the finished compost could be removed.

The size and expense of the Clivus Multrum made it unsuitable for use by homesteaders. Compost bins provided a more useful model. The idea was that if household wastes could be successfully composted in bins, human wastes could be, too. So Sim designed a household composting privy based on the compost-bin design, using concrete-block walls and a slab instead of the wood frame and removeable slats of the compost bin. The first composter was built in a house at Green Gulch Farm, a Buddhist retreat in nearby Marin County. Soon Sim's neighbor built one, and people started calling for plans. The virtues of the system were that it saved ten to fifteen thousand gallons of water that otherwise would disappear down each toilet every year; it reduced the need for large leach fields, and it literally made people responsible for their own shit, an idea that was attractive to libertarians, organic purists, outlaw builders, and people engaged in reexamining and redesigning all the aspects of their daily lives.

In many rural counties, the compost privy caught on like wildfire, and local health departments winced. For years, the official measure of material progress in the United States had been the number of flush toilets as counted by the Census. Now the steady, certain move forward was being threatened by an organic indoor outhouse! Moreover, the new design threatened established rules and regulations. Some environmentalists counted on conventional standards for septic tank/leaching-field systems based on water use to restrict new development. The building code defined habitable dwellings as having flush toilets and having electrical outlets every twelve feet. The regulations governing waste disposal allowed for alternatives, but no one ever asked about them.

Some time afterward, Sim's position as California State Architect and director of the state Office of Appropriate Technology allowed him to examine outmoded and inappropriate regulations. A major study of the health risks associated with compost privies was launched. The study found that they posed no health risks and also reported that the privies were safely collecting and storing waste materials even though the conditions required for optimal composting were not present in many of the units studied. Over the years, compost privies have come to be used around the world. People have modified the design for use in cold climates and other special conditions, developed new ways to control moisture, and made various other design improvements.

FIRST PRINCIPLE: SOLUTIONS GROW FROM PLACE

The compost privy design in both the United States and Europe grew out of specific site conditions and limitations as well as the values of users. Today, many design opportunities and possibilities are sacrificed to the gods of centralization and standardization, the supposed economies of scale, and a simple ignorance of how one learns from a place. In many ways, conventional wisdom works against learning from place. For example, many localities forbid a person, even if he or she owns the land, from camping on it before building a permanent structure. Some of the most beautiful, appropriate, and frugal homes have been built by nonarchitects and noncraftspeople who grew their houses over time as they learned about the peculiarities of their site, developing precise knowledge of place and making original and unique design responses.

SECOND PRINCIPLE: ECOLOGICAL
ACCOUNTING INFORMS DESIGN

The impetus to develop a way to recycle human wastes that does not require their dilution and transport by water came from an understanding of the incredible extravagance of conventional wastewater systems. These systems waste vast quantities of water, nutrients, and energy; are extremely expensive; and cause damage to freshwater and ocean habitats. No conventional design is executed without a careful accounting of all economic costs. Likewise, no ecological design is executed without a careful accounting of all *ecological* costs, from resource depletion to pollution and habitat destruction. Tracing the full set of ecological impacts of a design is obviously a prerequisite for ameliorating those impacts.

### THIRD PRINCIPLE: DESIGN WITH NATURE

When garbage becomes compost, an essential structure within nature is revealed. In nature, materials are continuously broken into their basic components and rebuilt into new living forms. In the compost privy example, applying the example of decomposition in nature provided a design solution that was radically different from the conventional method. By working with the patterns and processes favored by the living world, we can dramatically reduce the ecological impacts of our designs. The main thing we have learned in our attempts to incorporate natural processes in design is that all participants—designers, builders, clients, and users—seem enriched and enlivened by the experience.

### FOURTH PRINCIPLE: EVERYONE IS A DESIGNER

The compost privy design evolved from listening to people with a problem. There was no "client," and there was no "job." A design evolved and was adopted because it fit the needs of a particular community of people with shared values and circumstances. Often in such instances the distinctions between designer, participant, and user vanish. The best design experiences occur when no one can claim credit for the solution— when the solution grows and evolves organically out of a particular situation, process, and pattern of communication.

FIFTH PRINCIPLE: MAKE NATURE VISIBLE

While the compost privy was designed to conserve water, recycle nutrients, protect fragile sites, and save money, its most lasting effect lies elsewhere. Almost every user we have encountered talks about the learning that took place as a result of building and using this technology. The experience was not always pleasant: there were sometimes strong smells and too much liquid, and the user had to make an effort to manage and turn the pile. "Flush and forget" technology does not encourage mindfulness or a sense of responsibility. Yet the response was overwhelmingly positive: Sim received more thoughtful letters and suggestions regarding the privy design than for any other project. The design required people's involvement, and that involvement necessarily connected them with their own biological processes.

NOTES

1. Wendell Berry, *Home Economics* (San Francisco: North Point Press, 1987), 146.
2. For more information on the compost privy, see *The Toilet Papers* by Sim Van der Ryn (Ecological Design Press, 1995: Suite 185, Ten Libertyship Way, Sausalito, CA 94965).

# SOLUTIONS GROW FROM PLACE

*Ecological design begins with the intimate knowledge of a particular place. Therefore, it is small-scale and direct, responsive to both local conditions and local people. If we are sensitive to the nuances of place, we can inhabit without destroying.*

## SUSTAINABILITY IN TRADITIONAL CULTURES

In the year 563, Saint Columba left Ireland in a tiny rowboat, carrying with him the kernel of Celtic Christianity. He eventually landed on Iona, a tiny island in the Inner Hebrides off the west coast of Scotland. Hiking Iona, one is struck by the intimacy bestowed upon the landscape. Every hill, pond, beach, cove, bay, offshore rock, and cottage carries its history in its name. There is Dun'i, "Hill-Fort of Iona," with its little pond, Tobar na h'Atose, "the Well of Eternal Youth." Ancient marble and serpentine rocks can be found at Port Carnan a'Ghille, "the Port of the Young Lad's Rock." Garadh Dubh Staonaig, "the Black Dyke of Staonig," is a stone-and-earth running wall that glides over the contours of the land. Over the generations, cormorants have migrated across the sea to nest at Uahm nan Sgarhe, "the Cormorant's Cave."

The landscape of Iona is continually sung in the naming of its features. This intimate knowledge of place—of sacred springs, nesting cormorants, and ancient rocks—is the starting point for ecological design. It is *local* knowledge, attuned to the particulars of place.

Traditional place-centered cultures depended on their immediate surroundings for almost everything: water, food, shelter, materials, fuel, medicines, and spiritual sustenance. Instead of denying this interdependence with the living world, they celebrated it. Sustainability, built on patterns of long-term survival, was woven into the texture of everyday life. In the words of the Tewa Pueblo educator Gregory Cajete, "In each place, Native Americans actively engaged their respective environments, and in this engagement became participants with everything in their place. They affected their places and understood that their effect had to be accomplished with humility, understanding, and respect for the sacredness of their place and all living things of that place."[1] Stories, rituals, and rules gave members of these cultures detailed knowledge of their places.

This knowledge grows organically from a place itself. The poet Gary Snyder expresses it well: You "hear histories of the people who are your neighbors and tales involving rocks, streams, mountains, and trees that are all within your sight. The myths of world-creation tell you how *that mountain* was created and how *that peninsula* came to be there."[2] This knowledge provides the skills to take the pulse of place and foster its health. It concerns the creatures one meets on daily travels, the water one drinks, the trails one hikes. It is accessible to all, gradually accumulated over a lifetime of learning.

Unfortunately, we have largely lost touch with the particular knowledge of particular places, and the result is the placeless sprawl visible from any highway. "For most Americans," says Snyder, "to reflect on 'home place' would be an unfamiliar exercise. Few today can announce themselves as someone *from* somewhere. Almost nobody spends a lifetime in the same valley, working alongside the people they knew as children."[3] Ecological design requires us to once again engage our places, their joys and idiosyncrasies, their wind and water, their pulse and history.

Jerry Mander's book *In the Absence of the Sacred: The Failure of Technology and the Survival of the Indian Nations* makes a strong case for the survival value of indigenous knowledge systems. Mander tells an instructive story about Inuit caribou hunting on the Ellesmere Islands of Arctic Canada. Conventionally trained government wildlife managers told the Inuit to hunt only large or male caribou. The Inuit argued that this would be catastrophic for the herds, but their opinion went unheeded. The Inuit prediction turned out to be accurate. Despite a far lower hunting limit than that of the previous year, the population dropped dramatically.

The Inuit hunters knew that in a harsh environment, older and larger animals are critical for a group's survival. They have the experience and physical strength necessary to dig through the winter snow for food. The Inuit knowledge is grounded in careful observation of caribou behavior and is an appropriate basis for the ongoing stewardship of the caribou herd. As Mander concludes, "The sum total of the community's empirically based knowledge is awesome in breadth and detail, and often stands in marked contrast to the attenuated data available from scientific studies of these same populations."[4] Given this level of care, it is perhaps less surprising that the Inuit have managed to survive for thousands of years in a difficult and fragile Arctic land.

One of the ancient cultures of the Pacific Northwest, the Kwaakiutl, practiced a remarkable form of "logging" that took wood from a living tree. When a tree was cut, "it was considered 'killed,' but a standing tree from which boards were taken had been 'begged from.' The straight-grained trunk was notched 3 feet above the ground, then further up to the length of the desired boards. As the top notch was widened, yew wood wedges were pounded into the gap and down the sides, then a lever was worked from the upper split to the bottom, freeing the new board without killing the tree."[5] Contrast this simple, humble practice with the destructive clear-cutting now bleeding life from the old-growth forests of the Pacific Northwest. Clear-cuts leave a lunar landscape, a treeless wasteland no longer able to keep soil in place or support wildlife. The difference between the two logging practices—"begging" from a standing tree and clear-cutting—is the difference between a fundamentally sustainable culture and a fundamentally unsustainable one.

The botanist Gary Nabhan has spent many years documenting the subtleties of indigenous agricultural systems in Mexico and the United States. These systems are exquisitely responsive to place, manifesting a rich knowledge of local soils, animals, climate, hydrology, and plant genetics. They often feature local crop varieties, called heirlooms, representing "distinctive plant populations, adapted over centuries to specific microclimates and soils. They have been selected also to fit certain ethnic agricultural conditions; the field designs, densities, and crop mixes in which they have been consistently grown."[6] For instance, Hopi blue corn is structurally suited to deep, eight-to-twelve-inch plantings in sand, at a level where moisture is available. This enables the corn to flourish in the difficult conditions of the Southwest.

Traditional agricultural systems typically enhance genetic diversity through well-established cultural practices. Nabhan stresses the importance of these practices: "Since heirloom vegetables are by definition those passed generation to generation through family or clan, they are best represented in cultural communities where a thread of continuity has woven through the centuries."[7] Over many generations of plants and people, a careful partnership between nature and culture allows hardy varieties to coevolve to meet the vagaries of the environment. In this way, cultural diversity and biological diversity are inextricably linked.

In many forests in India, local knowledge of native trees and their multiple roles has allowed an effective integrated system of agriculture and forestry. Trees are cut only sparingly, since the role of their roots in soil and water conservation is well recognized. Leaves and small branches are used for cooking, as well as for green manure and animal fodder. Medicines are gathered, fruits are eaten, and seeds are made into oils. Trunks and large branches are used for housing, commercial firewood, and timber, and for the construction of carts and agricultural implements.

Yet these forests rich in tamarind and pongmia, jack and mango, are rapidly being replaced with eucalyptus monocultures. The range of original benefits from the forest is being reduced to a single cash crop: commercial timber. Why? The knowledge system with power, in this case "scientific forestry," does not acknowledge the value of any forest productivity that does not take the form of marketable timber. While the foresters speak only of profits on timber, the response of the locals is "What do the forests bear? Soil, water and pure air!" Scientific forestry, unlike the local knowledge of the forest dwellers, "splits forestry from agriculture."[8] In the same way, we have allowed engineering, architecture, and other design disciplines to be split from the very local knowledge systems that need to inform them.

As these examples illustrate, traditional cultures have achieved their longevity by structuring the smallest details of everyday life around the need to maintain the integrity of the ecosystems upon which they depend. Since these cultures are closely bound to a particular piece of land, actions have local, rather than global, consequences. If ecological limits are approached, it is possible to draw back because they are immediately perceived in the form of catastrophic resource losses. Hunting rights can be temporarily revoked, or land can be left fallow for a time. Sustaining the health of land, season after season, requires constant adjustment, care, and appropriate forms of knowledge.

In the late twentieth century, there is a deep desire to regain a balance between culture and nature, to put certain pernicious technologies back in the bottle, and to question every aspect of the contemporary landscape. We cannot do this without making bridges to the ecological wisdom inherent in the practices of traditional cultures. As Cajete suggests, "Indigenous people have demonstrated a way of knowing and relating that must be regained and adapted to a contemporary setting."[9] It is vital that we adapt traditional skills for respecting and preserving place to the possibilities and constraints inherent in our own technological culture.

### BRINGING SUSTAINABILITY HOME

The skills required to build a sustainable community are already actively employed in our everyday activities. It is simply a matter of applying them in the right way. Imagine attending to water, energy, waste, and land as carefully as you would attend to your garden, your children's education, or your money. If these skills are part of the fabric of everyday life, building sustainable communities is possible. It is one thing to read about some distant ecological calamity, and it is another to walk the land, see eroding streambanks, and bring the problem to the attention of the community. Sustainability begins in modest acts of responsibility.

In Berkeley, California, a group called Urban Ecology has begun to make the city streets speak of the land hidden beneath their surface. The Urban Ecologists have stenciled "creek critters"—frogs, salamanders, salmon, and other creek species—on streets above culverted creeks and painted the unambiguous warning "NO DUMPING—DRAINS TO BAY!" next to storm drains around the city. One can no longer dump motor oil down a drain without remembering that it goes to a creek and finally out to the San Francisco Bay. In a way, these stencils and warnings recall the deep reverence for *this* creek or *that* mountain intrinsic to traditional cultures. The citizens of Berkeley once culverted their creeks and buried their drainage systems, but now some other citizens are recalling these hidden veins, trying to be responsible for their health, and making others think of them.

Each such act, as modest as it may seem, contributes to a *culture of sustainability*—a shared awareness that can serve to regenerate the health of both people and ecosystems. We have already inherited the knowledge for creating such a culture of sustainability in the ecological wisdom embodied in traditional cultures. This wisdom can take root even in a highly technological culture if it is consciously nourished, cherished, and allowed to count for knowledge. Since sustainability is a cultural process, it depends on the everyday actions of ordinary people.

As we grow better at integrating sustainability into our daily lives, we will begin to find patterns of awareness and action that are analogous to those of the Inuit hunters or Hopi cultivators and yet are appropriate to our own situations.[10] These patterns can inform us and offer us guidance, much as ancient stories and rituals have always done. If we re-create these patterns in a sufficiently rich way, they can perform several critical roles simultaneously: They can restore our ability to perceive health and non-health in ourselves and our places so that we may have some basis for judging the efficacy of our actions. They can break down the tyranny of inaccessible technical language and allow communities to work on difficult issues in a fully participatory way. They can strengthen, rather than weaken, our confidence in our immediate experiences so that we can speak from the heart about our own perceptions.

To the extent that sustainability is imposed by outside forces, it will fail. Sustainability cannot be mechanically replicated under different conditions. It will take endless forms, the very diversity of design possibilities helping to ensure that the whole patchwork quilt of technologies, cultures, and values is sustainable. Bringing sustainability home is about growing a culture of sustainability that is suited to the particularities of place.

## VALUING LOCAL KNOWLEDGE

Local knowledge is valuable because it is appropriate. It is exactly what the Inuit need to live with the caribou or the Hopi to grow corn. It provides specific information about the climate, plants, trees, animals, water flows, and everything else making up the texture of a place. If we are to minimize destructive ecological impacts in our designs, it is precisely this kind of knowledge that we need.

One of us once heard a story about a Chilean farmer's wife. Tasting her freshly made butter one day, she noticed that it was a little sour. Just from the taste of the butter, she knew the problem lay in the cow's diet and was able to recommend to her husband appropriate crops to correct the field's nutrient imbalance. Imagine cultivating a similar sensitivity in our engineering, in our building, in our agriculture!

Local knowledge may be found in the stories that make up a place. In his rich book *The Dream of the Earth,* the monk Thomas Berry celebrates the bioregional story of his own home, Riverdale, which lies in the Hudson River valley:

> Tell me the story of the river and the valley and the streams and wood-
> lands and wetlands, of the shellfish and finfish. Tell me a story. A story
> of where we are and how we got here and the characters and roles that
> we play. Tell me a story, a story that will be my story as well as the story
> of everyone and everything about me, the story that brings us together
> in a valley community, a story that brings together the human com-
> munity with every living being in the valley, a story that brings us to-
> gether under the arc of the great blue sky in the day and the starry
> heavens at night, a story that will drench us with rain and dry us in the
> wind, a story told by humans to one another that will also be the story
> that the wood thrush sings in the thicket, the story that the river recites
> in its downward journey, the story that Storm King Mountain images
> forth in the fullness of its grandeur.[11]

Solutions grow from place, out of these stories pollinated by the generations, by the blending of human nature and wild nature. As our stories are told afresh, our places begin again to inform our decisions and our designs. In the Mattole watershed in Northern California, locals have been working for many years to enhance the failing salmon run. They have designed their own hatch boxes, carried out extensive creek restoration efforts, and planted thousands of trees. A generation of elementary-school children has released salmon into the wild as part of a watershed-based curriculum. The testimony of participant Freeman House is eloquent: "The salmon group worked from the assumption that no one was better positioned to take on the challenge than the people who inhabited the place. Who else had the special and place-specific knowledge that the locals had? Who else could ever be expected to care enough to work the sporadic hours at odd times of the night and day for little or no pay?"[12]

Local knowledge is best earned through a steady process of cultural accretion. The knowledge of the careful farmer or rancher, with his or her long experience of soil, crops, livestock, and weather, is an irreplaceable design resource. So is the knowledge of a traditional earth builder, a craftsperson, a fisherman, a bird watcher, or a rower. The collective memories of those who inhabit a place provide a powerful map of its constraints and possibilities. In a sense, ecological design is really just the unfolding of place through the hearts and minds of its inhabitants. It embraces the realization that needs can be met in the potentialities of the landscape and the skills already present in a community.

Sustainability is embedded in processes that occur over very long periods of time and are not always visually obvious. It follows that ecological design works best with people committed to a particular place and the kinds of local knowledge that grow from that place. This knowledge is slowly accumulated, season by season, through active engagement with the land. It concerns the humble details of a place, the smell of a field after the first fall rain, the derelict factory down the road, the cycles of decay and renewal, the surprise of previously unnoticed wildflowers. This knowledge is the prerequisite for maintaining cultural and biological diversity both within a local community and in wider habitats. Without local knowledge, places erode.

## RESPONDING TO COMPLEXITY

Back in the late 1980s, there was a strong push for Star Wars, a blanket of satellites that could shoot down enemy missiles in a nuclear war. The scheme relied on all kinds of fancy technologies including X-ray lasers, advanced radar systems, and attack and counterattack satellites. One of the most influential groups opposing the weapons system was the Computer Science Professionals for Social Responsibility (CSPSR). Their argument was simple: Given that a ten-line computer program probably won't work properly the first time through, how can a weapons system requiring ten million lines of instructions ever be debugged? Testing such a program thoroughly is not possible because the exigencies of battle are numerous and unpredictable. CSPSR was arguing that Star Wars would not work because of the unmanageable complexities inherent in its design.

There are limits to knowledge and therefore limits to management. David W. Orr puts it this way: "The ecological knowledge and level of attention necessary to good farming limits the size of farms. Beyond that limit, the 'eyes to acres' ratio is insufficient for land husbandry. At some larger scale it becomes harder to detect subtle differences in soil types, changes in plant communities and wildlife habitat, and variations in topography and microclimate. The memory of past events like floods and droughts fades. As scale increases, the farmer becomes a manager who must simplify complexity and homogenize differences in order to control."[13] Stewardship is quite different from management: it requires wisdom, restraint, and, above all, a commitment to and understanding of a particular place. Without enough "eyes to acres," stewardship is impossible. Careful attention to detail is lost in the rush to control ever larger and more unwieldy systems.

The emerging science of *complex systems* gives us a sobering perspective from which to view our own managerial crisis of complexity. Complex systems routinely undergo vast reconfigurations and realignments. Chaos theory tells us that even if we have an *exact* and *deterministic* model of a system that is completely closed to outside influences, we may have no hope of predicting its behavior beyond a certain time scale. The systems we deal with as decision makers and citizens are messier: We have imprecise models with lots of built-in randomness and plenty of outside influences. Without enough "eyes to acres," we will be unable to respond effectively to subtle ecological feedback. We may be tempted to homogenize differences in order to control and manage complexity.

To understand the implications of chaos, let's begin with the solar system. Hidden in Newton's deterministic, clockwork model of gravitational interactions is a long-term unpredictability. Computer simulations suggest that a single pebble passing through the fringes of the solar system will dramatically change planetary orbits over the course of millions of years. In other words, within this clockwork solar system lies the potential for the slightest perturbation to become vastly magnified. If we place Earth but a hair off course, that deviation will eventually be compounded to millions of miles. In a similar way, a butterfly flapping its wings in Madagascar can cause a hailstorm in Kansas two months later. This *butterfly effect* is inherently scale linking, allowing microscopic interactions to be amplified until they affect events even at a large scale. The microcosmos and the macrocosmos interpenetrate.

Since the butterfly effect renders *exact* long-term prediction impossible, we need to ask new kinds of questions. We can use the butterfly effect as a way of understanding our own crisis of complexity. Very tangible policy issues around fisheries, forests, greenhouse emissions, and so on are infused with so much complexity that we cannot hope to model them accurately enough to yield precise, certifiable results. When we compound a system's intrinsic capacity for enormously complex behavior with our own uncertain, incomplete models, we are left with a partial understanding at best. Perhaps we can peg a variable within wide limits or find certain loose correlations, but we are unlikely to be able to provide rigorous answers to key management questions. What climatic response can we expect from such-and-such level of carbon dioxide emissions? Is this truly a sustainable timber yield? The new sciences of complexity, far from increasing our confidence in answering such questions, are really telling us that systems are more delicate than we thought they were, and that guarantees of safety for our environmental interventions will be difficult to find.

The limits to knowledge implied by complex systems suggest that we cannot scientifically "manage" systems beyond a certain scale. Without a sufficient "eyes to acres" ratio, we will be overwhelmed by complexity. Hence, a vital role is opened for those on the land to participate in decisions at all levels. The understanding we need to restore and work with ecosystems of all kinds is distributed among those who know those ecosystems well. Indian scientist and activist Vandana Shiva puts it this way: "The ordinary Indian woman who worships the *tulsi* plant worships the cosmic as symbolized in the plant. The peasants who treat seeds as sacred, see in them the connection to the universe. . . . In most sustainable traditional cultures, the great and the small have been linked so that limits, restraints, responsibilities are always transparent and cannot be externalized. The great exists in the small and hence every act has not only global but cosmic implications."[14] Humble local acts, each respecting the whole web of life, add up to a sustainable culture.

To increase the "eyes to acres" ratio, we need to change the way we think about knowledge and design. We need to scale our designs both to the limits of ecosystems *and* to the limits of human understanding. This has the immediate advantage of bringing sophisticated forms of local knowledge into play. In turn, this local knowledge can inform the design process, providing it a high level of ecological sensitivity and appropriateness.


DESIGNING FOR PLACE

Only a few generations ago, it would have been absurd to suggest that one should design and build in ways that did not reflect local climate, materials, landforms, and customs. The design of human habitat was limited to local resources, abilities, and ways of doing things. Buildings tended to follow patterns that were well adapted to local conditions. Designing with and for place was the rule and not the exception.

Examples are provided by the indigenous domestic architecture that has developed in each climatic region. Desert villages across the world are built of thick walls of mud or stone with small windows, features designed to maintain cool interior temperatures. The dwellings are tightly clustered to shade each other. Huts in tropical deltas and forests are often raised up on stilts, providing welcome breezes and protection from the wet ground. Walls are woven and roof is thatched from local leaves such as palm. Roofs are steep to shed rain. The dwellings that evolved in the temperate forests of Europe and North America were built of logs and timbers, with steep roofs and overhangs to shed rain and snow. The nomadic herders of the plains of Asia, Africa, and North America evolved portable shelters consisting of light wooden frames covered with a double insulating wall constructed of animal skins.

In this century, tried and tested design adaptations to place have been abandoned in favor of standardized modern templates designed to be conveniently dropped into any situation and any location. As we have seen, these templates require extravagant amounts of energy and materials and destroy landscapes wholesale. They also erode local and regional differences. As the twentieth century comes to a close, places and cultures are being bulldozed into a planetary geography of nowhere. In this destructive context, the task of ecological design is to re-create design solutions deeply adapted to place. Both the lessons of indigenous design and sophisticated new ecological technologies are critical to this task.

An example of this approach is provided by an unbuilt design for the Ojai Foundation School by Sim Van der Ryn & Associates (figures 4–6). Ojai is about an hour's drive east of Santa Barbara on the central California coast. The climate—hot, dry summers and mild winters—is typical of an interior Mediterranean valley. The site, a saddle on a grassy ridge, was located through a consensual community process in which

FIGURE 4. *Model photo of Ojai Foundation School*

FIGURE 5. *Overall section of Ojai Foundation School*

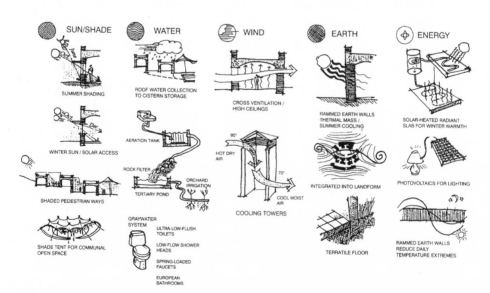

FIGURE 6. *Special features of Ojai Foundation School*

members silently walked the land until each found the spot that felt best to them. The program called for a "learning village" including student rooms, faculty residences, office, library, kitchen, dining area, and meditation hall. The plan is organized around a large central elliptical common space. Tiers of housing are arrayed on the south side of the ellipse with each tier shading the other. Common facilities are placed on the north side. The basic building material is soil excavated on-site. Six to 12 percent Portland cement (or fly ash, a waste product of electric power plants) is added, and the mixture is pneumatically rammed into reinforced formwork to make a two-foot-thick, durable, earthquake-resistant wall. This technology—known as rammed earth or pisé—is a modern adaptation of an approach used in China, Europe, and North Africa for centuries. The thick walls provide a thermal barrier that keeps interior rooms cool in hot weather.

The Ojai project also incorporates a passive cooling tower based on an ancient design. Throughout the Middle East, breezes were caught in towers and channeled over water pools to create a simple form of evaporative cooling. The Environmental Research Laboratory at the University of Arizona has developed an improved version of this design. A small amount of water is misted through baffles at the top of the tower to cool the air, which then flows down to the tower's base in a constant, refreshing stream.

Water is scarce in Ojai, an area with low annual rainfall. Rain falling on the rooftops is channeled to a concrete reservoir under the common area, where it is stored for later use to irrigate the orchard and garden. The plumbing system sends sewage to a septic tank and recycles kitchen and bath water (graywater) in the garden. The low electrical demand is provided on-site through photovoltaic arrays.

A very different response to a very different place is demonstrated in Sim Van der Ryn & Associates' design for the Lindisfarne Assocation Center in Crestone, Colorado. Located in the foothills of the Sangre de Cristo Mountains in southern Colorado, the site experiences extremely cold, windy, but sunny days in winter and a short, warm summer. Place prescribed a design that both maximizes the warming winter sun and minimizes the freezing winter winds. The design is a long, south-facing rectangle with lots of glass. The north wall and roof, both heavily insulated, are covered with soil to reduce the effect of wind and to stabilize temperature. The basic materials are primarily local rubble stone dumped into forms and pine timbers harvested from local trees killed by bark beetles. In spite of extreme winters in which wind chill can reach –60 degrees Fahrenheit, the space, heated only with an energy-efficient wood stove, remains above 55 degrees. This design makes extensive use of passive solar principles and technologies. Simple tools now available allow designers to predict year-round sun and shade patterns at a given site.

Ecological design begins with the particularities of place—the climate, topography, soils, water, plants and animals, flows of energy and materials, and other factors. The task is to *integrate* the design with these conditions in a way that respects the health of the place. The design works when it articulates new relationships within a context that preserves the relevant ecological structure.[15]

Consider wetlands. Their internal processes enable them to absorb nutrients, detoxify substances, and remove pathogens. Artificial wetlands—known as *constructed wetlands*—are now being seeded and maintained specifically to purify wastewater. When a constructed wetland is carefully matched to the level and type of wastewater it will receive, it can both reclaim nutrients and provide exceptionally clean water. In this way, some of our own wastes can be integrated within existing ecological cycles. The constructed wetland creates a new waste/landscape relationship that keeps nutrients on-site, prevents downstream water from being polluted, and provides additional habitat.

Ecological design works with the inherent integrities of a given place, recognizing that the extent to which we rely on far-flung resources is the extent to which we are no longer accountable to our own place. It is possible to temporarily live far beyond our local means, but only at the expense of destructive ecological subsidies from somewhere else. According to the plant geneticist Wes Jackson, we are "unlikely to achieve anything close to sustainability in any area unless we work for the broader goal of becoming native in the modern world, and that means becoming native to our places in a coherent community that is in turn embedded in the ecological realities of its surrounding landscape."[16] By integrating design within the limits of place—as in the case of constructed wetlands—we make it respond to these ecological realities.

Twenty years ago, solar architect Steve Baer pointed out the "clothesline paradox": We drill for oil in Alaska, send it through pipelines, refine it, and ship it to an oil-fired electrical utility. The oil is burned, producing steam to push turbines that generate electricity. The electricity is sent out to the grid, traveling hundreds of miles with transmission losses along the way, and thence to your clothes dryer. Here the electrical energy is converted to the mechanical energy of the revolving drum and the thermal energy of the heating coil in your dryer, allowing your clothes to dry. On the other hand, you could have just hung your clothes out to dry on a clothesline!

The clothesline paradox is a good metaphor for our inability to perceive locally available solutions. The clothesline replaces reliance on a distant and ecologically unsound energy system with an everyday ambient resource: warm air. In the same way, ecological design replaces conventional resource-intensive approaches with information-rich, locally adapted solutions. We begin with the particularities of place and ask, What can be done with ecological integrity here? How can we provide energy in this region? How can we provide water without adversely affecting hydrological cycles? How can we provide shelter without destroying forests?

Of course, the solutions will vary strongly from place to place. It is a matter of listening to *what the land wants to be.* It is said that in order to restore native vegetation, one begins with the area where it is most strongly established. Weed out non-native species, making space for the natives. In a few seasons, the range of the natives will increase, and they will bring their own propitious microclimate with them, eventually allowing them to recover much of their original vigor. It is a simple method, predicated only on a knowledge of local vegetation. In a similar way, ecological design seeks to gradually restore the healthy functioning of the landscape by allowing its original processes to return.

We are not proposing some kind of stylistic "regionalism" in design. We are speaking of paying rigorous attention—in the design process itself—to flows of matter and energy, to the characteristics of soil and climate, and even to the subtleties of habitat. Choosing to honor the integrity of ecological processes places strong constraints on design, and these constraints must be met *locally* as well as regionally and globally. By doing this, we can create systems that mesh so closely with nature's own regenerative processes that they begin to actively participate in them.

The common camel exemplifies the appropriateness to place that pervades nature's own evolutionary design. In the early morning, the camel browses vegetation for moisture. Some of this water is metabolically stored for later use in its fat layer, which doubles as a highly effective thermal insulator. During the day, the camel's own body is used as a thermal mass, and its temperature is allowed to increase to a threshold unusually high for mammals. Throughout this process, the camel minimizes water loss by producing concentrated urine. When the upper threshold of body temperature is reached, a special adaptation allows the camel to dry out while maintaining the health of its blood cells. When the temperature finally drops, the fat layer can be concentrated in the camel's humps, reducing its insulating effect and permitting faster cooling.

The camel's various adaptations—metabolic water from fat, concentrated urine, variable body temperature, low water loss in blood, humps—allow it to function effectively in the harsh desert climate. The camel, through its very physiology, can withstand extremes of temperature that would kill most organisms. It is exquisitely adapted to place.[17]

In contrast, sealed, centrally heated office buildings are like ostriches with their heads in the sand, doing everything but responding to place. If we begin to think of buildings themselves as *organisms* with functional relationships to their environment, new possibilities emerge. In designer

Day Chahroudi's vision, the building is a "one-celled organism whose environment contains all the necessary nutrients and also some hostile elements. . . . Using the selective permeability of its roof or walls the building exhibits homeostasis, perhaps the most basic property of living things."[18] The selective permeability is obtained by coating the inside of an ordinary window with a heat-reflective layer. The window lets in light but traps reradiated heat. This helps to allow a building, with proper solar orientation, to adapt itself to the local climate. In such a design, the harsh walls favored by industrial designers become softened to biological membranes, echoing the camel's adaptations. The building stays warmer in cold weather and cooler in warm weather.

Knowing the details of local climate is often the key to place-responsive architectural design. The Bateson Building in Sacramento was designed by the Office of the California State Architect with the explicit goal of reducing energy consumption by 75 percent (figures 7 and 8). In most office buildings, the biggest energy requirements are for artificial lighting and air conditioning. The Bateson Building relies primarily on daylighting through a floor plan in which no desk is more than forty feet from a natural source of light. A careful study of climate data showed that while the city often experienced a week of days over one hundred degrees during the summer, evening temperatures dipped into the fifties because of cool air creeping up the Sacramento River from San Francisco Bay. This became the heart of the climatic design strategy. The square-block building was designed around a large, four-story atrium under which was placed hundreds of tons of rock. During summer days, the building's heat is absorbed by the thermal mass of the rock. At night, large fans flush the thermal energy stored in the rock out into the cool evening air. The building is also provided with motorized shades that block incoming sunlight as necessary.

Just as the camel fits its desert niche and well-designed solar buildings fit their climates, ecological designs fit their places in rich and surprising ways. The knowledge needed to create them is inevitably place-specific.

FIGURE 7. *Exterior of Bateson Building*

Already in the 1940s, Lewis Mumford proposed anchoring education at all levels with a kind of "regional survey." This survey becomes "the backbone of a drastically revised method of study, in which every aspect of the sciences and the arts is ecologically related from the bottom up, in which they connect directly and constantly in the student's experience of his region and his community."[19] It embraces a careful study of both the local environment and the businesses, institutions, and people that make up a place.

In Austin, Texas, Pliny Fisk and the Center for Maximum Potential Building Systems (Max's Pot) have rigorously pursued the implications of Mumford's "regional survey." Max's Pot's most fully realized project to date is the Laredo Demonstration Blueprint Farm, a two-acre farm at the edge of Laredo, Texas. This project responds to the climate, mineral re-

FIGURE 8. *Courtyard of Bateson Building*

sources, vegetation, and soil of its region, which lies in a transition zone between the arid Southwest and the prairie grasslands. The farm, located near the Rio Grande, features a small orchard, shaded areas for growing, several storage sheds, cisterns, wind generators, and an on-site treatment system for agricultural wastes.

Max's Pot begins every project by looking to the ecologically appropriate designs indigenous to other *biomes*—biological regions—around the globe that have a similar climate and vegetation (figure 9). In Texas, the scrubby mesquite tree is regarded as a nuisance and ruthlessly cleared away. In the badlands of Argentina, though, it has long been used for floor tiles. On the Laredo farm, mesquite tiles are used for permeable paving. In a similar fashion, the farm's cooling towers in the storage sheds—similar to those in the Ojai design—were borrowed from Iran.

Max's Pot seeks regionally appropriate building systems that are "predicated on the uniqueness of place."[20] These systems catalyze local economies because they create local jobs right from materials extraction through processing and actual construction. At the farm, crops are shaded by a flexible network of poles, cables, and polyester panels. The poles are old oil-rig drilling stems found in a nearby junkyard. The farm's sheds were built with straw bales, a readily available agricultural waste. The roof supports are a clever latticework of locally fabricated thin steel trusses and decking. Concrete floor slabs will soon be mixed on-site with the locally available minerals pozzolan, lime, and caliche.

The design of the Laredo farm clearly grows from place, responding to the area's unique constellation of factors: Generators utilize the wind, cistern catchment systems capture rainfall, the crop-shading system and

FIGURE 9. *Biomes similar to Laredo's*

cooling towers provide protection from the sun, and agricultural wastes are treated before reaching the Rio Grande. It also uses local resources— vegetation (mesquite tiles) and minerals (caliche, lime, pozzolan, iron trusses)—and locally produced wastes (straw bales). Max's Pot is "mining for the knowledge to capitalize on local resources . . . and local farmers, metalworkers, and builders to sustain the small Blueprint Farm community and, by extension, dozens of such settlements on the periphery of existing cities."[21] By responding in an information-rich, energy-poor, and materials-frugal manner to a demanding landscape, the Laredo farm minimizes destructive ecological impacts.

At a large scale, basic issues become imponderable puzzles. What "economic value" should be assigned to the biodiversity of a tropical forest? What is the "optimal" level of greenhouse gas emissions? In each case, we seek an overly simple quantitative answer to a swelter of complexity. When we return to a human scale, these problems begin to resolve themselves. Design is accountable to place when we can read the consequences of our actions right on the landscape. It is not accountable to place when it relies on hidden, far-off ecological subsidies ranging

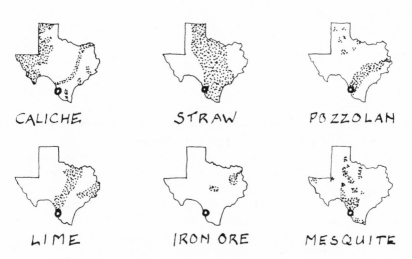

CALICHE  STRAW  POZZOLAN

LIME  IRON ORE  MESQUITE

FIGURE 10. *Distribution of building materials in Texas*

from the destruction of forests to the poisoning of waters and acidification of lakes. Neglect occurs in one place at the expense of intractable problems somewhere else. A project like the Laredo farm works because it is firmly grounded in the constraints and opportunities of a particular, well-defined region.

NOTES

 1. Gregory Cajete, *Look to the Mountain: An Ecology of Indigenous Education* (Durango, Colo.: Kivaki Press, 1994), 87.
 2. Gary Snyder, *The Practice of the Wild* (San Francisco: North Point Press, 1990), 26.
 3. Ibid., 25.
 4. Jerry Mander, *In the Absence of the Sacred: The Failure of Technology and the Survival of the Indian Nations* (San Francisco: Sierra Club Books, 1991), 258–9.
 5. Peter Nabokov and Robert Easton, *Native American Architecture* (New York: Oxford Univ. Press, 1989), 247.
 6. Gary Paul Nabhan, *Enduring Seeds: Native American Agriculture and Wild Plant Conservation* (San Francisco: North Point Press, 1989), 71.
 7. Ibid., 72.
 8. Vandana Shiva, *Monocultures of the Mind: Perspectives on Biodiversity and Biotechnology* (London: Zed Books, 1993), 14.
 9. Cajete, *Look to the Mountain*, 79.
10. We are indebted to Katy Langstaff for her provocative notion of a "pattern for sustainability."
11. Thomas Berry, *The Dream of the Earth* (San Francisco: Sierra Club Books, 1990), 171–2.
12. Freeman House, "To Learn the Things We Need to Know: Engaging the Particulars of the Planet's Recovery," in *Home! A Bioregional Reader*, ed. Van Andruss et al. (Gabriola Island, British Columbia: New Society Publishers, 1990), 112.
13. David W. Orr, *Ecological Literacy: Education and the Transition to a Postmodern World* (Albany: State Univ. of New York Press, 1992), 35–6.
14. Vandana Shiva, "The Greening of the Global Reach," in *Global Ecology: A New Arena of Political Conflict*, ed. Wolfgang Sachs (London: Zed Books, 1993), 154.
15. Thanks to Katy Langstaff for some helpful discussions on the related notion of structure-preserving transformations.
16. Wes Jackson, *Becoming Native to This Place* (Lexington: Univ. Press of Kentucky, 1994), 3.

17. See R. J. Putman and S. D. Wratten, *Principles of Ecology* (Berkeley and Los Angeles: Univ. of California Press, 1984), 40–1.

18. Day Chahroudi, "Buildings as Organisms," in *Soft-Tech,* ed. J. Baldwin and Stewart Brand (London: Penguin Books, 1978), 43.

19. Lewis Mumford, *Values for Survival* (New York: Harcourt, Brace & Co., 1946), 151–2.

20. John Todd originated this phrase.

21. Ray Don Tilley, "Blueprint for Survival," *Architecture* 80, no. 5 (May 1991): 70.

# ECOLOGICAL ACCOUNTING INFORMS DESIGN

*Trace the environmental impacts of existing or proposed designs. Use this information to determine the most ecologically sound design possibility.*

## ECOLOGICAL ACCOUNTING

All of us are familiar with the conventions of economic accounting. No design gets very far without accompanying budgets, spreadsheets, parts lists, and so forth. Unfortunately, we have largely failed to consider the parallel set of accounts that link designs to the health of ecosystems. These accounts cover acres of abused land, kilowatt-hours of energy, gallons of water, pounds of eroded soil, and all the other environmental impacts of a design. Just as standard accounting procedures allow us to determine how money is acquired and spent, ecological accounting procedures provide a way of tracking ecologically relevant variables.

For several decades, ecologists have produced detailed studies of the flow of energy and materials through ecosystems. Ecological accounting requires us to do the same for products, buildings, landscapes, and entire communities. As Wes Jackson observes, sustainability will result from "our becoming better ecological accountants at the community level. If we must as a future necessity recycle essentially all materials and run on sunlight, then our future will depend on accounting as the most important and interesting discipline."[1] Careful ecological accounting provides an accurate measure of the environmental impacts of designs, allowing these impacts to inform the design process.

Suppose the Acme factory upriver is polluting your favorite fishing hole. While the factory may be within its legal emissions limit, its activities nevertheless have a direct bearing on the health of the river and your enjoyment of it. The pollution, even though free for the polluter, represents a cost to you. In the language of economics, the pollution is an *externality;* that is, it impacts only third parties not directly involved in buying and selling Acme's products.

Externalities create a tension between economic accounting and ecological accounting. In a world rife with externalities—from acid rain to global warming and ozone depletion—minimizing economic costs often maximizes environmental and social costs borne in the form of pollution, habitat destruction, and sickness. Market prices fail to reflect wider environmental costs because those costs do not show up in conventional economic accounting. There are few markets in clean air, water, and soil.

Ecological accounting is a way of gathering information for making design decisions in the absence of prices that accurately reflect overall ecological costs. Consider the greenhouse emissions associated with petroleum fuels. While the 1973 OPEC embargo raised the specter of petroleum scarcity, the 1990s have raised the equally disturbing specter of petroleum abundance. As a strong scientific consensus on the greenhouse effect now indicates, continuing present rates of fossil fuel consumption will lead to an increase of five to ten degrees Fahrenheit in global mean temperature by the midpoint of the next century. This will lead to massive crop failures, catastrophic monsoons in Southeast Asia, loss of vast ranges of habitat, and a host of presently unpredictable side effects.

The consensus greenhouse scenario is so disturbing that it can only be considered a threat to global security. Meanwhile, U.S. emissions of carbon dioxide are not taxed or regulated in any significant way even though steep energy taxes have sharply reduced energy consumption in Europe and Japan. Petroleum prices provide a textbook example of the inability of markets alone to guarantee a livable future. While markets accurately reflect supply and demand, they are clearly insufficient to ensure the environmental preconditions for life on this planet.

If prices reflected underlying environmental impacts, there would be plenty of incentive to design products that were ecologically sound. In such a system, these products would end up being *cheaper,* not more expensive. Paul Hawken has proposed such a system in *The Ecology of Commerce:* "To create an enduring society, we will need a system of commerce and production where each and every act is inherently sustainable and restorative. . . . Just as every act in an industrial society leads to environmental degradation, regardless of intention, we must design a system where the opposite is true, where doing good is like falling off a log, where the natural, everyday acts of work and life accumulate into a better world as a matter of course, not a matter of conscious altruism."[2]

In the absence of such a sensibly designed system of commerce, ecologically sound products come to market at a higher price than their destructive counterparts. Everyday acts, like purchasing pesticide-laden produce, have effects that are hidden to the purchaser. Without consulting an ecological shopping guide or deliberately looking for produce that is "certified organic," one may unintentionally promote an essentially dysfunctional economy. The onus is placed on the careful choices of informed consumers who are willing to pay more to decrease their own environmental impacts.

The gap between economic accounting and ecological accounting presents an exciting challenge for ecological designers. When minimizing environmental impacts coincides with saving money, as in the case of many energy- and water-efficiency measures, the choice is clear. When minimizing impacts seems to require greater expense, as in the case of nontoxic finishes or paints, the choice becomes more complicated. How much extra money should be spent for what level of reduced impact?

Ecological design brings these considerations to the forefront of the design process. It asks us to *explicitly* consider the environmental impacts of everything we include in a design, from the energy use of a building to the toxicity of a product. The goal is then to improve the ecological accounts—by decreasing energy and materials use, reducing toxicity, and lessening other impacts—while maintaining a sensible budget. Often the large cost savings from one set of ecologically sound design choices can help offset the extra expenses associated with another set. In other cases, design decisions that are individually more expensive may yield a synergistic effect that makes them collectively cheaper. For instance, a highly effective passive solar design might pay for itself by eliminating the need for central heating and cooling systems.

Ecological accounting begins with a careful choice of accounts. Typical accounts cover the type and quantity of energy, water, materials, toxins, wastes, and land used in a design. In an agricultural context, we might pay particular attention to energy, water, land, soil, and key nutrients. In an office building, energy, building materials, and toxins would require special scrutiny. In a product design, energy, materials, toxins, and wastes would be most important. These accounts can be kept with varying levels of precision, but they should reflect—at least qualitatively—the most significant environmental impacts incurred by a design.

Ecological accounting also requires us to choose boundaries of space and time for our inquiry. If we trace all of the impacts of a design over its complete history, we are performing *life-cycle analysis*. In this case, discussed in the next section, we sum impacts over the lifetime of a design. In the final section, "Following the Flows," we examine the flows of resources needed to sustain a given building, campus, or town in its daily operations. In both cases, a consistent, meaningful choice of boundaries helps to focus the ecological accounting procedure and lend it greater relevance to the design problem at hand.

Suppose we were to set up the ecological accounts for two familiar processes: gasoline combustion and photosynthesis. Let us represent a process—respiration, combustion, distillation, and so on—by a circle. Inputs like steel, oxygen, energy, and water are shown by an arrow entering the circle. Outputs, including both useful products and wastes, are shown by an arrow leaving the circle. With these conventions, gasoline combustion and photosynthesis may be depicted as in figures 11 and 12.

Industrial processes like gasoline combustion typically manifest a single century or less of human design ingenuity. These processes often accomplish their narrow objectives well, but at great ecological cost. Usually, they are resource intensive, running at very high temperatures and pressures. Their waste products include substances so toxic that they are dangerous even at a level of one part per *billion* or less. While the processes of nature have been tested over geological time and of necessity fit with the fabric of life, industrial processes have severe impacts that can be reduced only through a conscious design effort.

In the case of gasoline combustion, the energy-rich fuel is derived from millions of years of photosynthetic activity. When one gallon of gasoline is burned, it produces twenty pounds of carbon dioxide as well as trace quantities of other substances like nitrogen and sulfur oxides and ozone. When this process is replicated in thousands of cars driving around a city, it results in smog and regional acid rain. When it is replicated in millions of cars all over the planet, it results in a massive contribution to the greenhouse effect.

Industrial processes are extravagant in their use of energy and materials and dangerous in their production of wastes. In contrast, nature's own metabolic processes, like photosynthesis and fermentation, are frugal and pollution free. Indeed, "compared with the elegance and

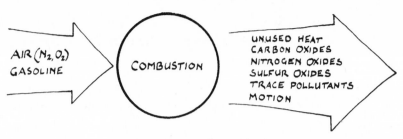

FIGURE 11. *Gasoline combustion*

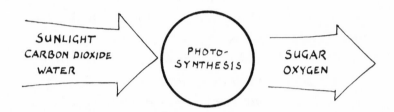

FIGURE 12. *Photosynthesis*

economy of biological processes . . . most existing industrial processes appear to be far from their potential ultimate efficiency in terms of the basic chemical and energy pathways they use."[3] While nitrogen-fixing bacteria quietly perform their work in the soil, we require three hundred times standard pressure and temperatures upwards of eight hundred degrees Fahrenheit to accomplish the same purpose in fertilizer plants.

In photosynthesis, carbon dioxide, sunlight, and water are transformed into a common sugar, dextrose. Photosynthesis is a remarkably elegant process, one that took three billion years of evolutionary design to perfect. It converts a common waste product of respiration (carbon dioxide) into two vital substances, sugar and oxygen. Unlike gasoline combustion, photosynthesis produces no waste products. It runs at everyday temperatures and pressures and is fueled by sunlight and water. Not surprisingly, ecological accounting greatly favors photosynthesis over gasoline combustion!

All processes must obey two simple laws of energy accounting. The first law tells us that the energy stored in the inputs must equal the energy stored in the outputs plus any waste energy. In the case of gasoline combustion, the chemical energy stored in the gasoline is converted to the mechanical energy of the piston together with waste heat.

The second law tells us that energy degrades in quality or usefulness as it is converted from one form to another. While the chemical energy of gasoline can easily be released at any time with a match, the dispersed heat energy from combustion can be only partially recovered. In any process, energy will become decreasingly available for further use, or, equivalently, *entropy* will increase.

These two laws form the backbone of thermodynamics, and they have been helping engineers and physicists work with energetic transformations for more than a century. Twenty years ago, Amory Lovins, a physicist by training, applied these laws to the entire energy system of the United States. He realized that "people do not want electricity or oil, nor such economic abstractions as 'residential services,' but rather comfortable rooms, light, vehicular motion, food, tables, and other real things. Such end-use needs can be classified by the physical nature of the task to be done."[4] He argued that the quality of energy supply should be matched to its end use, for example, keeping a room comfortable or running a motor. To use a high-quality energy source, such as electricity, for a low-quality end use, such as heating the leaky bag of air we call a house, was entropically insane, much like cutting butter with a nuclear-powered chainsaw. His radical pronouncements in the 1970s—"Stop living in sieves," "Stop driving petropigs"—have been translated into policy in many countries.

In *Soft Energy Paths,* Lovins was able to show that U.S. electricity consumption could be cut drastically without sacrificing any end-use benefits. The key is *efficiency:* fewer steps in the energy delivery process, each better designed to minimize wasted energy. The arithmetic is clear: The overall efficiency is the product of the efficiencies at each step. If each step is 70 percent efficient, and this is an optimistic figure, then a three-step process will be just 34 percent efficient, and a five-step process just 17 percent efficient.

If the overall efficiency increases, then the level of end-use benefits may be maintained even as the energy input declines. Lovins has shown that if all Americans adopted the highest-efficiency refrigerators available instead of their present masterpieces of dumb design, the energy saved would allow two dozen nuclear reactors to be shut down. He has also been able to show utilities and their regulators that meeting demand through efficiency is cheaper than increasing supply. Outfitting customers with energy-efficient lights is more sensible, both economically and environmentally, than building a new coal-fired utility.

There are already burgeoning markets in energy efficiency or *negawatts*. A negawatt, or negative watt, is a unit of *decreased energy demand*, just as a conventional watt is a unit of increased energy supply. Electrical utilities or large customers can purchase decreased energy loads—i.e., negawatts—from energy services companies (ESCOs) that provide them through a clever combination of high-efficiency lights, motors, and appliances; physical plant improvements; weatherproofing; and so on. One common arrangement is for an ESCO to offer to split the energy savings with a business. The ESCO purchases and installs the appropriate energy-saving equipment for the customer. The ESCO pays for the installation and maintenance of the equipment itself; its return is a reasonable share of the energy savings resulting from these changes. The customer bears no risk and gets solid energy savings without spending hundreds of hours doing research on energy efficiency. We may hope for eventual markets in negagallons of water, negatons of toxic waste, and negabarrels of oil!

All processes must also obey a fundamental law of materials accounting: matter is neither created nor destroyed. If a carbon atom enters the process, a carbon atom must leave the process. This law tells us that the carbon and sulfur in gasoline must be accounted for in a car's emissions. The carbon is emitted largely as carbon dioxide, while the sulfur is emitted in the form of oxides contributing to acid rain. Matter that fails to appear in useful products must contribute to the waste stream: there is no other possibility. A great deal of useful information can be obtained by carefully balancing the materials accounts.

In an effort to address materials accounting, many nations are now scrambling to set up a system of national ecological accounts. These accounts attempt to quantify the natural wealth—forests, minerals, air, soil, water, and so on—upon which their economic wealth depends. A World Resources Institute case study of Indonesia from 1971 to 1984 demonstrates this idea. Although Indonesia's gross national product increased by 7.1 percent annually, adjustments for resource losses—depletion of petroleum reserves, forests, and soils—lowered the growth rate to just 4 percent. Indonesia's efforts to rapidly "mine" its own natural wealth resulted in a burst of apparent economic growth that might well cripple its own long-term economic prospects.[5]

Ecological accounting—whether at the level of an industrial process, product, building, community, or nation—provides a coherent framework for assessing environmental impacts. It allows us to think more carefully about the connections between ecology and design. Ecological accounting is the key analytical tool of ecological design, for it provides a kind of litmus test for sustainability.

### LIFE-CYCLE ANALYSIS

Each object has a history of its own. Your favorite chair, for example, probably was made from wood harvested hundreds of miles away in a logging operation that entailed a network of fellers, roads, and trucks. From there, the wood was milled and sent to a factory for assembly into a chair. At the factory, resins, adhesives, and varnishes were applied as the chair took form. Finally, the chair was packaged, shipped, warehoused, shipped, retailed, and brought home. In several decades, it will probably grow quite rickety, at which time its owner can repair it, junk it, or salvage it in some way.

In a deep sense, the chair embodies the materials, energy, water, and land used during its production and distribution. In other words, these impacts need to be charged against its ecological accounts. The chair is connected, in a tangible way, to the health of streams, forests, and mountains across North America. The Vietnamese monk Thich Nhat Hanh expresses it this way: "When we look at a chair, we see the wood, but we fail to observe the tree, the forest, the carpenter, or our own mind. When we meditate on it, we can see the entire universe in all its interwoven and interdependent relations in the chair. The presence of the wood reveals the presence of the tree. The presence of the leaf reveals the presence of the sun."[6] Ecological design recognizes that all problems—hence, all solutions—spring from this connectedness.

Looking at environmental impacts over time, we are led to examine the entire histories of the things we use. We need to understand the processes responsible for their creation and decide whether they conserve or squander materials and energy, whether they are toxic or benign, and whether they enhance or diminish the health of those who do the work at each stage. Ecological design demands that we ask of everything we use, "What was sacrificed to create it? What harm to people, animals, and nature was caused by its creation? Or was it created with love which helped people, animals and nature along the way? That is, we have to ask very hard questions of the economic process and we have to apply human and ecological values. . . . Can we now, fully informed, lay claim to this thing and love this thing?"[7] This kind of life-cycle analysis revolves around a detailed understanding of the impacts incurred during an entire life-cycle, from the extraction of raw materials through manufacturing, use, and eventual recycling or discarding.

Peter Bahouth, the current director of the Turner Foundation, has gone to some trouble to research and write a kind of ecological biography of a typical North American tomato that begins to suggest the environmental ramifications of industrial agriculture. He calls it "The North American Regional Report, or the Attack of the Killer Tomato," and addresses it to "nervous eaters."[8]

As Bahouth describes it, the tomato was grown on Mexican land traditionally used by Mexican farmers involved in cooperatives, or *ejidos*.
The seed was a hybrid—based on a Mexican strain—now patented by a
genetic engineering firm that relied on taxpayer-funded research by the
University of California, Davis. The land was fumigated with methyl-
bromide, one of the most ozone-depleting chemicals in existence. It was
then inundated with toxic pesticides. The production waste from the pesticide manufacturing process was sent to the world's largest toxic dump
in Emelle, Alabama, which happens to sit next to a poor African American community.

Mexican farmworkers, displaced from the *ejidos,* were given no protection from the pesticides they applied. Nor were they given any in-
struction in the proper application of these dangerous substances. The
workers make about $2.50 a day and have no access to health care.

The tomato was put on a plastic tray, covered in plastic wrap, and then
placed in cardboard boxes. The plastic was manufactured with chlorine
from Point Comfort, Texas. Residents of Point Comfort face manifold
health effects from exposure to dioxins, extremely toxic byproducts of
chlorine manufacture. The cardboard began as part of a 300-year-old ancient forest in British Columbia, was processed in the Great Lakes, and
was then shipped by the United Trucking Company to Latin American
farms. The whole process was fueled by oil from the Gulf of Campeche,
Mexico, extracted by Chevron and processed by PEMEX, the Mexican
national oil company.

The boxed tomatoes themselves were artificially ripened by applying
ether. Now tasteless and nutritionally impaired, the tomatoes were sent
by refrigerated trucks throughout the continent. The trucks and distribution centers rely on ozone-depleting CFC cooling equipment. Finally,
the tomato arrived, weary and watery, in the salad on *your* plate.

Bahouth's tomato was not deliberately chosen as a particularly destructive product. Performing some ecological accounting for this tomato, he
uncovered a vast web of environmental side effects ranging from ozone

depletion to dioxin contamination to global warming. The life-cycle of an orange, toothbrush, or appointment book would reveal a similar web of effects. While Bahouth's tomato does not single-handedly destroy cultures, disfigure landscapes, or change the climate, it is an integral part of a system that does all of these things. The damage is done slowly, cumulatively, through a series of small failures of design and conscience.

The Environmental Protection Agency has already set up a formal life-cycle analysis project for use in regulating products and processes.[9] This project is attempting to standardize life-cycle analysis methodology so that it can used by industry and government alike. One of its prototype examples is a bar of soap, which turns out to be implicated in a surprisingly complex web of processes. Its ingredients include sodium hydroxide, tallow, chemicals, pigments, and fragrances. Sodium hydroxide leads us to a rock-salt mining process, and tallow to the cattle industry. In fact, the entire soap manufacturing process is just the beginning of another series of processes extending from packaging to retailing and consuming.

A life-cycle analysis like this one is an exemplary kind of ecological accounting. It reveals the relative impacts of the various stages of economic activity, from resource extraction through manufacturing, distributing, retailing, consuming, and discarding. Further, it is a tool for making ecologically sound choices. Since purchasing a product indirectly supports all the steps in its life-cycle, it is important to know how destructive these steps are.

Recent German legislation has taken life-cycle analysis from the theoretical to the practical. It requires auto manufacturers to take back each car they make and completely recycle its component parts. This legislation creates a direct incentive for a new kind of design that reclaims as much value as possible when a car is disassembled. It has spurred a move toward using fewer different materials and more modular design than before, so that a car can be more easily broken into useful elements when it is recycled. The car's "decay" and reintegration into the industrial system become design considerations right from the start.

This attempt to design-in the recycling of the various materials making up a product is termed *design for disassembly*. Such design intelligently anticipates and facilitates recycling and reuse. It directly reduces the need for virgin materials in the product's manufacture. In addition, remanufacturing recycled materials is much less energy intensive than manufacturing from scratch—95 percent less in the case of aluminum.

The German government is also seriously considering a proposal from the Hamburg-based Environmental Protection Encouragement Agency (EPEA) to make manufacturers fully responsible for the life-cycles of their products. The EPEA proposes that products be divided into three categories: consumption products, service products, and unmarketable products. Under this "Intelligent Products System," consumption products must be fully biodegradable and can be safely discarded after use. Service products—like television sets or automobiles—must be completely recycled by their manufacturers after they have served their functions. Unmarketable products cannot be safely used or disposed of. They must be chemically marked with the manufacturer's molecular signature and held for safekeeping in a waste "parking lot." In case of leaks or accidents, the offending chemicals will be traced back to their manufacturer, who will be severely penalized.[10]

In the United States, the American Institute of Architects (AIA) has been promoting a deeper awareness of materials, energy, and toxicity issues among architects. The following list of questions, adapted from the AIA's "Making A Difference: An Introduction to the Environmental Resource Guide," provides an example of life-cycle thinking in an architectural context:[11]

1. How much "embodied" energy does the building material create over its entire life?
2. How much energy is required to manufacture the material and related products?

3. How much energy is used in transporting the material from source to project site?

4. Are renewable or sustainable energy sources used in the manufacture of the material?

5. Are there less energy consuming, longer-lived alternatives for the same application?

6. Are local sources for the material available?

7. Can the material be recycled or reused at the end of its useful life in a structure?

8. How easy or difficult is the material to recycle?

9. Do different construction systems offer better opportunities for resource recovery at the end of building life?

10. How much maintenance does the material require over its life in a structure?

11. How energy intensive is the maintenance regimen?

12. Are waste byproducts produced during maintenance?

13. Does the material require special coatings or treatments that could present health or safety hazards?

14. If the material produces off-gasses during and after installation, how is indoor air quality affected?

15. Are hazardous solid, aqueous, or gaseous wastes produced during the manufacturing process environmentally significant?

16. How do the amounts of waste resulting from manufacture, fabrication, and installation compare with those from alternative materials?

These questions help us examine a building in a new way. For example, the second and third questions ask us to consider how much energy is required to extract, process, manufacture, and transport a building material. One recent study has provided quantitative estimates of this *embodied energy* for various materials. Wood has the least embodied energy, at 639 kilowatt-hours per ton. Brick is next (4 times the amount for wood), followed by concrete (5×), plastic (6×), glass (14×), steel (24×), and aluminum (126×).[12] The wide variation in embodied energy for different materials confirms that this an important design issue.

Ecological accounting can cause a painful shock of recognition: our own choices as consumers or designers implicate us in environmental impacts occurring, as often as not, a thousand miles away. In the words of the cartoon character Pogo, "We have met the enemy, and he is us." Identifying impacts, both qualitatively and quantitatively, is a way of improving our present practices. Clear ecological accounts help set the context for ecological design.

### FOLLOWING THE FLOWS

If we turn our ecological accounting to the resource flows—electricity, water, food, and so on—necessary to maintain a building, campus, or community, we grow more sensitive to the systems supporting our lives. Last fall, Sim ran a design studio that focused on the four San Francisco Bay Area hostels run by the American Youth Hostel Association. One group of students attempted to follow the flows of the downtown San Francisco hostel at Mason and O'Farrell Streets. They chose six areas of interest: electricity, garbage, natural gas, recycling, sewage, and water. For each area, they gave practical suggestions for hostelers, provided basic facts on environmental impacts, and mapped the wider resource flows that the hostel was participating in. They detailed their results in a series of multilingual (English, French, German, Spanish, and Japanese) presentation boards. It is worth summarizing the students' research here:

*Electricity.* The local utility, Pacific Gas and Electric Company, derives its electricity from a wide range of sources. These include imports from other utilities in the western states and Canada (25 percent), eight fossil-fuel plants just south of San Francisco (25 percent), a nuclear plant near San Luis Obispo (17 percent), seventy hydroelectric plants in the Sierra Nevada (8 percent), a geothermal plant about a hundred miles north of San Francisco (8 percent), and other sources including wind power from Altamont Pass and solar power from Death Valley (17 percent). This represents an unusually diverse range of sources.

*Garbage.* San Francisco generates twelve hundred tons of trash per day, which corresponds to eight pounds per person, almost twice the national average. This garbage is collected and trucked to a transfer station just south of the city. About one hundred large trucks carry the garbage seventy miles east to the Altamont Landfill. This huge landfill occupies 1,528 acres. There is a biogas recovery facility on-site that supplies more than six thousand homes.

*Natural Gas.* Pacific Gas and Electric's sources include California gas fields (11 percent), Alberta gas fields (51 percent), and southwestern gas fields (38 percent). The utility delivered about seven hundred billion cubic feet of natural gas in 1990.

*Recycling.* Used glass is melted and processed into new products in Oakland. Used plastic bottles are trucked to Chino in Southern California and remanufactured for a wide range of applications. Aluminum is shipped to Texas for processing. Most of the used paper and cardboard is sent to Pacific Rim countries and made into new paper and cardboard products.

*Sewage.* Each day, the Oceanside Treatment Plant dumps 22 million gallons of treated effluent four and a half miles out into the Pacific Ocean. The North Point Treatment Plant and the Southeast Treatment Plant dump 60 million gallons into San Francisco Bay. This works out to about 111 gallons of sewage per person.

*Water.* Water begins as snowmelt in the High Sierra. It passes through a complex system of regulating reservoirs and pipelines, is treated, and is eventually stored in municipal reservoirs.

The educational value of following the flows is immense. It is a practical, ethically engaged way of understanding the ecological implications of design. A recent issue of *New Directions for Higher Education,* "The Campus and Environmental Responsibility," presents a series of case studies in which students and faculty have traced resource flows at various universities: UCLA, Tufts, Brown, the University of Kansas, the University of Wisconsin–Madison, Hendrix College, and others. In the issue, David W. Orr suggests the creation of a curriculum focusing on this activity: "The study of institutional resource flows suggests a non-traditional pedagogy that involves students in matters that are direct, tangible, immediate, and consequential. In the food studies . . . students participated in every step, all the way through the preparation of the proposals that went to the respective college administrations. In the process, students learned how their institutions worked; they learned about agriculture, economics, ecology, and ethics; and they learned that they were implicated in food service systems that were neither sustainable nor just."[13] Such a nontraditional curriculum would emphasize active involvement in environmental decision making.

One of the earliest studies of campus ecology occurred at Arkansas' Hendrix College in 1986. Four students, under the direction of Orr's Meadowcreek Project, spent a summer tracking down the sources of the food served in the school's cafeteria. Armed with notepads and a video camera, the students traveled the country documenting their food suppliers. They discovered that only 6 percent of the cafeteria's food came from Arkansas, a state with a strong agricultural base.

Vegetables and fruit traveled two thousand miles from California, with a corresponding loss of nutritional value. Growers in California "admitted to the students that their products were developed to survive the long truck ride, and there was little concern for the nutritional quality."[14] Freezing, canning, and packing in chemical preservatives also did little to enhance the quality of the produce. Furthermore, "while beef cattle grazed within sight of campus, the meat served on campus came from a large feedlot operation in Texas. Since cattle raised under the stressful conditions of confinement in a feedlot do not have the same flavor as range-fed beef, fat from Iowa was added to the meat to improve the taste, and then the beef was shipped to the campus."[15] The imperatives of the campus food-services industry had placed a premium on meals that were simple to prepare, not on meals that were nutritionally sound or bound to place.

In 1988–9, further funding was obtained to transform the buying habits of the campus food service. Local farmers were encouraged to grow food for the cafeteria, and the cooks were given additional training and help in developing menus that would incorporate the new food sources. The campus earned much goodwill in the local community because its purchases were a direct source of economic stimulation. Arkansas sources now account for 30 percent of all food purchased, up from 6 percent at the beginning of the study. Items prepared with local ingredients are labeled with a small emblem that indicates the food's source. In this study, following the flows of the food system opened the way to a less environmentally destructive system that supported local farmers and provided students with more nutritious food.

A new generation of ecologically engaged artists is busy making resource flows a tangible part of our lives. Just as the Hendrix cafeteria menu reminds students to consider the source of their food, the work of New York City artist Mierle Ukeles reminds us of our relationship to garbage. In 1977, Ukeles became the first artist-in-residence of the New York City Department of Sanitation. An early performance was the eleven-month-long *Touch Sanitation,* in which she shook the hands of all the sanitation workers in the city. Ukeles believes that

> the design of garbage should become the great public design of our age. I am talking about the whole picture: recycling facilities, transfer stations, trucks, landfills, receptacles, water treatment plants, rivers. They will be the giant clocks and thermometers of our age that tell the time and the health of the air, the earth and the water. They will be

utterly ambitious — our public cathedrals. For if we are to survive, they will be our symbols of survival.[16]

Since 1983, Ukeles has been working on a complex piece called *Flow City,* housed in the Marine Transfer Station at West Fifty-ninth Street along the Hudson River. At the transfer station, trucks deliver garbage to be barged across to Fresh Kills Landfill in Staten Island. The "Passage Ramp" presents a vast panorama of recycled art to the intrepid visitor. Along this ramp, "the materials of glass, metal, and plastic are separated, suspended, and composed in a spiraling format. . . . Ukeles' space introduces the concept that waste is a false cultural construct; every item is inherently valuable if only our traditional thinking about garbage can be changed."[17] At the end of the 248-foot passage, the visitor can walk out on the "Glass Bridge" to see trucks dumping their contents onto waiting barges. Ukeles describes this space as "the violent theater of dumping." The "Glass Bridge" terminates in the "Media Flow Wall," an installation of twenty-four video monitors displaying live and prerecorded images of the Hudson River, landfill operations and restoration efforts at Fresh Kills, and everyday recycling efforts. *Flow City* is a rich interpretation of New York City's waste stream that forces its visitors to rethink their relationship with garbage.

New applications of ecological accounting are also providing a way of relating resource flows to the landscapes that sustain us. William Rees, a professor in the School of Community and Regional Planning at the University of British Columbia in Vancouver, has attempted to calculate the land area it would require to *sustainably* provide the 1.7 million inhabitants of the Vancouver–Lower Fraser Valley Region with food, forest products, and fossil fuel. Rees estimates that it would take 2.7 acres to provide each inhabitant with an average Canadian diet, 1.2 acres with forest products, and 8.6 acres with renewable biomass production sufficient to replace current fossil fuel use. Multiplying 12.5 acres per capita by 1.7 million people, one finds that an area of 21 million acres is required to provide basic resources for the region—an area *twenty-two* times larger than the region itself.[18]

This kind of result challenges us to think more carefully about our patterns of consumption and practices of design. Ecological accounting encourages us to ask tough questions and seek detailed answers. Designs that minimize environmental impacts while meeting economic constraints cannot be developed without clear and comprehensive tools for assessing those impacts. Explicitly setting up accounts for energy, water, materials, and other key variables provides critical guidance for the ecological design process.

NOTES

1. Wes Jackson, *Becoming Native to This Place* (Lexington: Univ. Press of Kentucky, 1994), 99.

2. Paul Hawken, *The Ecology of Commerce: A Declaration of Sustainability* (New York: HarperCollins, 1993), xiv.

3. Hardin Tibbs, "Industrial Ecology: An Environmental Agenda for Industry," *Whole Earth Review*, no. 77 (winter 1992): 15.

4. Amory Lovins, *Soft Energy Paths* (New York: Harper & Row, 1977), 39.

5. World Resources Institute, *World Resources 1990–91* (New York: Oxford Univ. Press, 1992), 235.

6. Thich Nhat Hanh, *The Sun My Heart* (Berkeley: Parallax Press, 1988), 90.

7. Andrea Cowles, *Archipelago*, no. 1 (spring 1992): 14–15.

8. Peter Bahouth, *Seeds of Change* catalog (Santa Fe, N.Mex.: 1994), 61.

9. This example is from Joel Makower, *The E Factor: The Bottom-Line Approach to Environmentally Responsible Business* (New York: Random House, 1993), 44.

10. Michael Braungart and Justus Engelfried, "The Intelligent Products System," *Bulletin of the Environmental Protection Encouragement Agency* (1993).

11. Guidelines from the AIA presented in *Architecture* 80, no. 5 (May 1991): 118.

12. John Tillman Lyle, *Regenerative Design for Sustainable Development* (New York: John Wiley & Sons, 1994), 119.

13. David W. Orr, "The Problem of Education," *New Directions for Higher Education*, no. 77 (spring 1992): 6.

14. Gary L. Valen, "Hendrix College Local Food Project," *New Directions for Higher Education*, no. 77 (spring 1992): 79.

15. Ibid.

16. Quotation of Mierle Ukeles is from Barbara Matilsky, *Fragile Ecologies: Contemporary Artists' Interpretations and Solutions* (New York: Rizzoli, 1992), 78.
17. Ibid., 76.
18. William E. Rees and Mathis Wackernagel, "Ecological Footprints and Appropriated Carrying Capacity: Measuring the Natural Capital Requirements of the Human Economy," in *Investing in Natural Capital: The Ecological Economics Approach to Sustainability,* ed. AnnMari Jansson et al. (Washington, D.C.: Island Press, 1994), 370–1.

# DESIGN WITH NATURE

*By working with living processes, we respect the needs
of all species while meeting our own. Engaging in
processes that regenerate rather than deplete, we
become more alive.*

## A PARTNERSHIP WITH NATURE

Evolution generates many levels of wholeness simultaneously, from the metabolic dance of a cell to the vast cycles maintaining the biosphere. These nested levels of integrity are sustained by their own characteristic patterns of health. By designing *with* nature, by working with these patterns of health, we may aspire to designs that are compatible with the living world.

Each level of integrity manifests a working logic of its own. The cell lives in relation to its neighbors, exchanging signals and nutrients. A community of organisms is woven together by cooperation and competition, by food webs and habitat. The biosphere itself pulses with the interconnection of all life. Each level — cell, organism, ecosystem, bioregion, biosphere — presents a series of critical design opportunities and constraints.

Designing with nature is a strategy for successively reducing harmful impacts by attending to the preconditions of health for each level. This philosophy of design represents more than a shift in language and epistemology: it is a shift in the way things are made and landscapes are used. Designing with nature acknowledges that in the long run, the most ecologically benign solutions make the most active use of life's own patterns of health.

These patterns, honed by life and time, cannot be easily enumerated. There is no end to the work of discerning them or to the work of translating them into designs that are both effective and culturally appropriate. They are as inexhaustible as nature's own generative capacities. Designing with nature suggests an ongoing partnership with nature, one that benefits both people and ecosystems.

We are in nature, and nature is in us. We face an interesting ambiguity of "multiple perspectives, of design as pattern, of ourselves as nature's designer and nature's designs."[1] This suggests that ecological design is a result of our constructive engagement with nature. It reflects nature's underlying integrities, finding within them a new context for design.

Ecological design is predicated on the coevolution of nature and culture. It is a kind of covenant between human communities and other living communities: Nothing in the design should violate the wider integrities of nature.[2] We are currently breaking this covenant at every level. We are re-engineering the genetic instructions of a single cell, killing off entire species, even disturbing the climate.

The case of toxic substances is instructive. While these substances are common in nature, they are highly specific, produced in small quantities as needed, and completely biodegradable. Rattlesnake venom is produced at the point of application, inside the snake. It is not produced centrally and shipped cross-country in venom trucks and railcars, with spills threatening entire ecosystems.[3] By choosing to work with toxic substances unfamiliar and destructive to the living world, we are breaking our covenant with nature.

In his seminal book *Design with Nature,* Ian McHarg wrote that "our eyes do not divide us from the world, but unite us with it. Let this be known to be true. Let us then abandon the simplicity of separation and give unity its due. Let us abandon the self-mutilation which has been our way and give expression to the potential harmony of man-nature."[4] This harmony clearly must respect each level of evolutionary design integrity. For instance, in our dealings with an ecosystem, we ought to match flows of materials to its assimilative capacities, preserve critical habitat, and in every possible way respect the patterns responsible for its continuing vitality.

While this harmony clearly has the negative value of a constraint— "Do not transgress this limit," "Do not harm this piece of land"—it is also an endlessly fertile source of solutions. The designs that most deeply reflect this harmony are themselves an active part of it, not just mimicking nature in an abstract sense, but participating in a living dance in a health-giving way. Nature is not a model for designs that are then kept rigidly apart in a purely cultural realm. Nature is a matrix *within which* designs find an identity and a coherence that contribute to the health of the whole. Ecological designs are articulated within an ecosystem or bioregion in the way veins are articulated within a leaf. They fill out an existing structure in a way that enhances the life, the flows, the processes within it.

This chapter explores some of the implications of designing with nature. It is intended to provide a flicker of illumination, a brief exploration of some favorite examples. The discussion is suggestive rather than exhaustive, for the design possibilities opened up by a collaboration with nature are as unlimited as those employed by the living world itself.

### WASTE EQUALS FOOD

Walk through one of California's temperate rainforests and you will see fallen redwoods that have been feeding fungi and sheltering animals for a thousand years. Out of decay new trees spring forth. The forest community maintains its health century after century because every process of growth is linked to a process of decay.

It is no small thing for the complementary activities of millions of species to cycle elements from simple to complex forms and back again. The manifold compounds necessary for the redwood's survival are familiar foods for the microbes, fungi, insects, and plants that are nourished by its life and eventual decay. This cyclic and interdependent economy is intrinsically diverse and sustainable. It is predicated on frugality and regeneration.

In *Farming: A Hand Book,* Wendell Berry speaks of the farmer in this way:

> The grower of trees, the gardener, the man born to farming,
> whose hands reach into the ground and sprout,
> to him the soil is a divine drug. He enters into death
> yearly, and comes back rejoicing. He has seen the light lie down
> in the dung heap, and rise again in the corn.[5]

Sunlight is gathered by the grains, providing food for the cow, whose dung fertilizes the soil. In turn, the soil nurtures next year's corn. Each of nature's diverse ecosystems—from forest to farm to wetland—participates in restorative materials cycles that maintain the availability of all substances critical to life.

In contrast, our own economic processes are linear. We are transforming vast quantities of raw materials into dangerous pollutants. We are degrading materials, making them less and less available for future use. Stocks of fossil fuels and ores are being burned and dissipated. We are deeply altering the nutrient cycles that sustain all life. All this because we have not designed products and processes whose wastes can be reintegrated into the economy.

In nature, waste equals food. Plants transform water, carbon dioxide, and sunlight into sugars, and these sugars are broken back down by other species. Carbon atoms are reincarnated, now bound on the surface of a giraffe's skin, soon rolling across the fields as tumbleweed. Over a period of four billion years, there have always been niches for organisms that could make use of underutilized chemical pathways. As these niches have filled, an extraordinarily efficient system of nutrient cycling has developed. While nutrients may be trapped for a time on the ocean floor or under layers of rocks, in geological time they are released. On average, there is virtually no net depletion of any nutrient.

If a community of organisms living in close association cannot jointly process their own wastes and cycle their nutrients, the association will not survive for long. Without continual cleansing and recycling, toxins rapidly accumulate and food disappears, eventually killing the community. In the same way, if a web of businesses working in close association cannot jointly utilize their waste streams and cycle their materials, the web will collapse. It will run out of resources and asphyxiate itself in a landscape of slag heaps and toxic dumps.

If businesses were able to turn waste into food, they could sharply reduce both pollution and the need for raw materials. Together they could form an *industrial ecology* that is fully integrated within wider natural cycles of materials. This industrial ecology would close the loops left open in conventional industrial processes. It would virtually eliminate irreversible flows of virgin materials into pollutants, transforming them into flows complementary to nature's own.

Closing the loops in industrial processes accomplishes two critical tasks. First, it turns waste into a resource, displacing the need for raw materials. Second, it avoids turning waste into pollution. Industrial ecology ensures that our choices of materials, processes, emissions, and ways of reclaiming waste are compatible with the integrity of ecosystems, watersheds, and the biosphere itself. Waste, *by design,* equals food. It either cycles back into industrial ecosystems or enters natural ecosystems in nontoxic forms at levels that can be properly assimilated.

One of the earliest formulations of industrial ecology was described in a 1989 *Scientific American* article written by two General Motors executives. They argued that "the traditional model of industrial activity—in which individual manufacturing processes take in raw materials and generate products to be sold plus waste to be disposed of—should be transformed into a more integrated model: an industrial ecosystem. In such a system the consumption of energy and materials is optimized, waste generation is minimized and the effluents of one process—whether they are spent catalysts from petroleum refining, fly and bottom ash from electric-power generation or discarded plastic containers from consumer products—serve as the raw material for another process."[6] Industrial ecosystems mimic the restorative materials cycles of natural ecosystems. They optimize the recycling and reuse of each material separately, but they also allow for the creation of more complex "food webs" of materials. Most important, they do not overwhelm their surrounding natural ecosystems with either the scale or toxicity of their pollutants.

Back in the Proterozoic era, about two billion years ago, the Earth witnessed a massive pollution crisis. Running out of easily available hydrogen sulfide fuel, early photosynthesizing cyanobacteria developed a more abundant substitute: water. They released oxygen liberated from water in copious quantities. Atmospheric oxygen quickly rose from one part in a million to one part in five, from a trace contaminant to a major component.

Oxygen, being an extremely volatile gas, posed difficulties for early life. Anaerobes literally decomposed on exposure to oxygen; they were driven underwater and underground. Yet, in a surprising reversal, they eventually developed respiration—the ability to use the very oxygen that had threatened them. Waste oxygen now fueled respiration. Oxygen levels were maintained at a constant level, and the oxygen crisis was averted.[7]

Our present pollution crisis also results from a failure in design. We are missing a whole metabolic level that could bring industrial processes back in balance with the living world. In a sense, we are waiting to discover the industrial analog of respiration!

All organisms turn energy and food into living matter while producing waste materials of various kinds. This waste matter becomes food for legions of saprophytes, literally "decay eaters." These decomposers, which outnumber species of all other kinds, include beetles, fungi, nematodes, and bacteria. Through their complementary metabolic pathways they return both essential nutrients and trace minerals to active circulation. Their role is a very important one, for without them, nutrients would rapidly dissipate. In many terrestrial communities, 90 percent or more of photosynthetic production passes directly to the decomposers.

While conventional industrial systems almost completely neglect them, the decomposers necessarily play an important role in industrial ecology. We need to design industrial ecosystems with processes of decay and breakdown explicitly in mind. As industrial consultant Hardin Tibbs observes, "Perhaps the key to creating industrial ecosystems is to reconceptualize wastes as products. This suggests not only the search for ways to reuse waste, but also the active selection of processes with readily reusable waste."[8] By failing to think clearly about processes of decay, whether of metal, plastic, food, or whatnot, we miss an opportunity to design with regeneration in mind.

A few years ago, a film studio in Wuxi, China, faced a difficult pollution problem: It was producing large quantities of silver-contaminated wastewater. The relatively low silver concentrations, under one part per million, prohibited the use of conventional chemical treatment and recovery. On the other hand, these concentrations were dangerously high for many aquatic organisms.

This waste lacked a complementary process of regeneration. It was a potential resource going unused. In response, the studio decided to create a series of living filters. Wastewater now meanders through ponds planted with water hyacinths *(Eichhornia crassipes)* and some other species of aquatic plants, spending about two or three days in treatment. The root system of the water hyacinth is an exceptionally fine silver filter. It can concentrate—"mine"—silver up to thirty-five thousand times its level in the wastewater.

When the roots are burned, the silver remains trapped in the ash. This ash can contain up to 4 percent silver, which represents a high grade of ore. The silver is extracted from the ash with standard methods, resulting in an overall retrieval rate of 95 to 99 percent. With a conventional treatment system, the silver would remain at unacceptably high levels in the effluent. Furthermore, the studio would be forced to purchase substantially more silver from external sources, causing further environmental destruction. Instead, this ecological wastewater treatment system produces clean water and allows silver to be recycled in an effective way. The water hyacinths ingeniously turn waste into "food."[9]

The conventional cleanup of toxic-waste sites is extremely expensive and often creates as much of a health hazard as it prevents. Polluted water, sludge, or soil is typically dredged and burned off-site. In the incineration process, many toxic substances are released. The alternative is to treat the wastes on-site with organisms chosen from an array of living filters, including bacteria, algae, fungi, and plants. This technique, called *bioremediation,* relies on the ability of organisms to break down, render less toxic, or sequester substances ranging from pesticides to heavy metals. Bioremediation is typically cheaper than conventional treatment and has the additional advantage of actually reclaiming sites rather than destroying them in the "cleanup" process.

Mel Chin, an artist with a longstanding concern for ecological issues, has been working with plants that can grow in heavily contaminated soil. Such plants are sometimes found near ancient European mine sites, where they have adapted over the centuries to high levels of toxicity. Remarkably, they can draw heavy metals up through their root systems. These plants, known as *hyperaccumulators,* can increase concentrations of metals like lead, zinc, and cadmium thousands of times, gradually detoxifying soils in the process. Chin was so intrigued with the purifying potential of the hyperaccumulators that he created a demonstration landfill cleanup project to highlight their abilities. He negotiated with various public agencies, finally obtaining permission to plant a sixty-foot plot by agreeing to undergo forty hours of hazardous materials incident response training.

The Pig's Eye Landfill in St. Paul, Minnesota, a state Superfund priority, is highly contaminated by cadmium and other heavy metals, mainly from old batteries. Chin and colleagues fenced a plot in the landfill and planted a hybrid variety of sweet corn *(Zea mays),* bladder campion *(Silene cucabalis),* and four other species. This was one of the first field tests of the hyperaccumulators, and it was a dramatic success. After a single growing season, the plants were cut and dried like hay, and then burned. The ash, like that of the water hyacinths at the Wuxi film studio, contained such large concentrations of heavy metals that it was of ore grade.

Chin's piece, appropriately named *Revival Field,* transcends merely symbolic concerns by actively engaging the health of ecosystems. Chin describes his piece this way: "The work, in its most complete incarnation (after the fences are removed and the toxic-laden weeds harvested), will offer minimal visual and formal effects. For a time, an intended invisible aesthetic will exist that can be measured scientifically by the quality of a revitalized earth. Eventually that aesthetic will be revealed in the return of growth to the soil."[10] Ironically, a National Endowment for the Arts grant for *Revival Field* was almost rescinded on the grounds that it was not "art"!

Chin is now working with an international team of artists and scientists to make the cleanup operation pay for itself. In effect, toxic sites will be "mined" for heavy metals by planting successive crops of hyperaccumulators. Each crop will be burned, and the metal recovered from the ash will be sold to finance the cleanup. In this case, the design solution relies on the inherent ability of certain plants to remove large quantities of heavy metals from the soil. With the right kinds of plants, a toxic site can gradually be restored to health.

Other applications of living filters are equally exciting. Recent NASA studies indicate that certain plants can effectively reduce indoor pollution levels by absorbing polluting gases into their leaves. Spider plants can remove carbon monoxide, aloe veras can remove formaldehyde, and chrysanthemums can remove benzene.[11] Water trickling over a moss surface creates an effective two-stage filtering system. The water absorbs and accumulates pollutants in the air, and the mosses, with their unusually large surface area, purify the water as it trickles past. The system also provides impressive levels of evaporative cooling.[12] Bacteria are being used to eat up oil spills, peat moss is refreshing stale office air, and fungi are cleaning contaminated soils.

Our own bloodstreams constantly exchange oxygen-rich red blood and waste-laden blue blood. There is much to learn by observing the transition from blue blood to red blood, from waste to nutrients. Waste is eliminated from one process in order to maintain its own integrity. It is then incorporated as a source of nutrients by a second process.

The flow of materials throughout a system is our source of inspiration as ecological designers. Since nutrients—useful materials—are valuable and wastes are costly, there is a huge incentive to figure out what process your waste is food for. "Waste" must always be understood as material of no value only to the process at hand, and not as material of no conceivable value to any process at any time.

A very literal application of the notion that waste equals food is provided by the waste and materials exchanges presently operating in several states. In the California Waste Exchange's *Directory of Industrial Recyclers and Listing of Hazardous Wastes Available for Recycling*, for example, are listings for both industrial recyclers and available hazardous wastes. Hazardous wastes are listed in the following categories: acids, alkalis, antifreeze, catalysts, caustics, coolants, dry-cleaning wastes, inorganics, metallic salts and sludges, metals (many categories), oils, oil filters, organics, solvents, transformers, waxes, and wood and paper. A typical recycling entry might include "waste acids, including chromic, hydrochloric, nitric, phosphoric, and sulfuric," and available wastes might include "phosphoric acid solution containing 5–10% phosphoric acid and 95% water generated from iron phosphate coating of computer panels."[13] Waste exchanges point toward an inevitable trend: matching wastes generated to available recycling processes. Instead of paying high fees for disposal, producers can sell wastes or pass them over to recyclers.

Unutilized wastes are actually a symptom of poor design. They can cause two kinds of pollution: toxic pollution and scale pollution. Toxic pollution includes traditional hazardous wastes with corresponding health risks to human communities and ecosystems. Scale pollution includes wastes—like carbon dioxide or CFCs—that are destructive only in their aggregate effects and not in small quantities. Scale pollution presents a severe design challenge. Indeed, writes Hardin Tibbs, "the scale of industrial pollution is now so great that even normally nontoxic emissions, like carbon dioxide, have become a serious threat to the global ecosystem. Seen in its broadest terms, the problem for our industrial system is that it is steadily growing larger in comparison with the natural environment, so that its outputs are reaching levels that are damaging because of their sheer volume, regardless of whether they are traditional pollutants or not."[14]

The Center for Maximum Potential Building Systems (Max's Pot) is currently testing new building materials and other products utilizing wastes. For example, when coal is burned, it produces large quantities of fly ash and sulfur dioxide. The fly ash can be used as an additive in concrete; the sulfur dioxide, which causes acid rain when released into the atmosphere, is already precipitated out so that coal utilities can meet emissions standards. The sulfur dioxide can easily be extracted from the precipitator stack, thereby providing a useful industrial feedstock chemical as well as another potential concrete additive. Sulfur can even be used as a natural pesticide to retard home insect infestation. Max's Pot is experimenting with other innovative materials, including waste straw for straw-bale houses and woodchips as a cement stabilizer.

We are just beginning to create full-fledged industrial ecosystems in which wastes from many different processes become food for others, and in which energy use and materials use are jointly optimized. The most fully realized example to date is in Kalundborg, Denmark (figure 13).[15] The project encompasses an electric-power plant (Asnaes), an oil refinery, a pharmaceutical plant, a wallboard factory, a sulfuric acid producer, cement manufacturers, local agriculture and aquaculture, and nearby houses. In the early 1980s, Asnaes started supplying excess steam to the refinery and the pharmaceutical plant. It also began supplying waste heat for a district heating system, allowing thirty-five hundred household oil furnaces to be shut off. In 1991, the refinery began removing sulfur from its gas, selling it to a sulfuric acid producer located in nearby Jutland. The wallboard factory was already buying surplus gas from the refinery, and the refinery's sulfur-reduction initiative made it possible for Asnaes to buy the remaining low-impurity gas.

Asnaes is now selling its fly ash to the cement manufacturer and will soon sell waste gypsum to the wallboard plant. Its waste heat is also sent to its own greenhouses and fish farm, which produces two hundred tons of trout and turbot a year. Other loops are closing fast: The refinery provides wastewater to Asnaes, and the pharmaceutical plant is turning its sludge into fertilizer for local farms. In Kalundborg, the deliberate reintegration of waste has greatly decreased environmental impacts.

Each of these examples of industrial cooperation was cost-effective and occurred spontaneously. In the case of Kalundborg, the benefits of coordinated activities are clear: Wastes become profitable intermediate products, and producers close enough to directly utilize the wastes can obtain a cheap source of supply. The possibilities for planned industrial ecosystems are even greater. If the metabolisms of several producers were

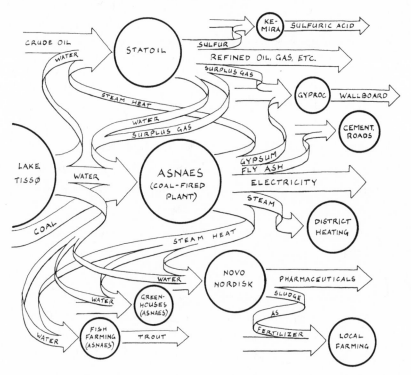

FIGURE 13. *Flows of materials and energy in the Kalundborg industrial ecosystem*

linked right from the design stage, it would be possible to minimize overall levels of materials, energy, and pollution. Each member of such a consortium would have lower costs because of the synergies inherent in the design.

The strategy of turning waste into food is an essential one if we are to fully integrate human activities within nature's own cycles. We have no choice but to replicate nature's own sunlight-driven regenerative cycling of materials. The extent to which we fail to close our own materials cycles is the extent to which we endanger nature's own. By converting linear, pollution-producing processes into interconnected cycles, we can vastly reduce the impact of everything we make and build.

ACTIVE LANDSCAPES

Joseph Needham, the great historian of Chinese science and civilization, tells an interesting story about the ancient debate between Confucian and Taoist water engineers. The Confucians favored strict control of water flow, a tradition clearly taken up by the Army Corps of Engineers in our own century. The Taoists believed that water should meander over the landscape, following its inherent tendencies. Reflecting on that belief, the Taoist engineer Chia Jiang wrote three thousand years ago, "Those who are good at controlling water give it the best opportunities to flow away."[16]

Then, as now, there was a struggle between the desire to make more land available for homes and agriculture and the desire to respect the integrity of existing hydrological cycles. In the compromises inevitable in practice, the narrow channels of the Confucians were often buttressed with retention basins for occasional floods. On the other hand, the very wide dikes of the Taoists were augmented with additional channels to allow farming during nonflood conditions.

The Taoist engineers were content to observe flows of water over the landscape and design accordingly. They saw the land as an *active landscape* providing ecological functions that simultaneously meet the needs of both people and wider living communities. They valued the intrinsic integrity of the landscape and found both meaning and sustenance by participating in its processes. In contrast, the Confucian engineers saw the need to discipline water, placing it in a position subordinate to the needs of civilization. They were also willing to expend vast amounts of labor and materials to reach this end.

We have responded to our own landscapes much as did the Confucian engineers. We have built vast water projects, destroyed wetlands, imposed systems of agriculture alien to the capacities of the land, and mined entire regions beyond recognition. We have not valued landscapes for their own sake, encouraging their own processes, instead seeking narrowly productive landscapes that are stripped of their wider ecological significance.

Ecological methods of flood control are currently experiencing a revival of interest. These methods rely on a healthy landscape in which vegetation moderates flow, erosion is minimized, and water is allowed to follow its own course. The goal is to restore ecosystems so that they can play their long-lost role of controlling flooding. By their design, these natural systems offer additional amenities like recreational areas, trails, and wildlife habitat. Furthermore, they are less prone to catastrophic failures like the great Mississippi floods of 1993.[17]

Ecological flood-control systems are a return to the idea of active landscapes. Thirty years ago, the ecologist Howard T. Odum did pioneering research on the energetic contribution made by natural systems in such processes as water purification. These contributions, though left unvalued in our usual accounting, often have a very high monetary equivalent. When they are added to well-recognized values like recreation or habitat, they provide a strong case for preserving the ecological integrity of the land.

The range and quality of these free services are astonishing. A recent study documents about two dozen functions supported by wetland systems alone.[18] Wetlands preserve genetic and community diversity and provide food and habitat for migrating birds and other creatures. Wetlands are nurseries for a wide range of aquatic organisms. They also attenuate floods, purify water, build soil from sediments, regulate groundwater recharge and discharge, and provide local and global climate stabilization. If these services could somehow be assigned monetary values, they would add up to a substantial figure. Ironically, wetlands are typically seen as having marginal value and are therefore convenient targets for development. As recent studies indicate, with a fuller ecological accounting, the true value of wetlands may be at least ten times their appraised value.

The ability of vegetation to moderate local climate is well established. A single tree can "provide the same cooling effect as ten room-size air-conditioners working twenty hours per day."[19] In Tucson, Arizona, the

Urban Releaf program aims to plant half a million desert-adapted trees over an eight-year period. Initial studies indicate that electricity savings from reduced demand for air conditioning will be more than five million dollars per year. A carefully maintained active landscape can also influence patterns of air flow, moderating pollution. Michael Hough reports in a recent article that the German city of Stuttgart "has retained the hills that surround the city for parkland and agriculture, because it has found that green hillsides greatly reduce air inversions and pollution problems by maintaining the free flow of katabatic winds that ventilate the city."[20]

Even a humble stormwater retention basin, designed to control urban runoff, can serve many other roles. At the West Davis Ponds in Davis, California, a flat, lifeless retention pond has been transformed into a rich source of habitat and recreation. Islands and pools shaped from the earth and planted with native vegetation are now attracting Canada geese, avocets, egrets, muskrats, and many other species. What is more, says landscape architect Robert L. Thayer, Jr., "by weaving the ecological structure and function of the [watershed] back into our neighborhoods, we are able not only to reinforce the community of humans, but also to rebuild the wider and truer community of all living creatures."[21] The basin has become a visible part of an active landscape.

The Arcata Marsh and Wildlife Sanctuary is a 154-acre wetlands park nestled between the Northern California town of Arcata and Humboldt Bay. With 220 recorded species, it offers the best bird watching around. On a busy day, the ponds are ringed with telescopes on tripods. It has become a favorite lunch spot for office workers and has attracted thousands of new tourists to the town of fifteen thousand.[22]

Walking around the flourishing marsh, one is surprised to discover that it is actually purifying the wastewater from the entire town. The marsh, constructed on derelict land, has been treating sewage from the town's conventional primary treatment plant since 1986. As the water meanders through the marsh over a two-month period, it is purified by plants like duckweed, cattails, pennywort, and bulrushes; aerobic and

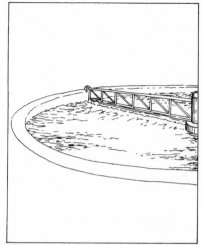

FIGURE 14. *Conventional wastewater treatment pond juxtaposed with constructed wetland*

anaerobic bacteria; mollusks; and fish. When the water is finally pumped from the marsh out to Humboldt Bay, it is generally of higher quality than the bay water itself.

The marsh has become a source of great civic pride. The town "inaugurated its new sewage system by holding a 'Flush with Pride' festival. Citizens wore T-shirts emblazoned with the festival's logo, a salmon leaping out of a toilet as a great blue heron perched on the seat."[23] The Arcata marsh carefully matches a human waste with an ecosystem for which the waste becomes a resource. The marsh has been designed as an active landscape that partially substitutes ecological intelligence for energy, materials, and dollars.

The Arcata marsh relies on the inherent purification abilities of healthy wetlands. In a similar way, we can create agricultural landscapes that mimic the structure and function of wild ecosystems. At the Land Institute in Salina, Kansas, Wes Jackson and his colleagues have been searching for a sustainable form of prairie agriculture in the image of a wild prairie. In this vision, agroecosystems, or agricultural ecosystems, "should mimic the vegetation structure of natural plant communities. This means developing agroecosystems that incorporate crops as structural mimics, and thereby functional analogs, of wild species. Cropping systems then would resemble, and behave like, natural communities."[24] If the structural mimics can successfully re-create their roles in wild ecosystems, then these agricultural ecosystems should inherit many of the ecological functions that lend stability to their wild counterparts.

The very pressures that caused prairie vegetation to evolve—an extreme climate ranging from -40 to 115 degrees Fahrenheit, fire, and large grazers—have lent it long-term resiliency. The prairie's diverse plant species seek water and nutrients at different soil depths. Their very diversity prevents the spread of diseases and pests. Copious legumes continually add nitrogen to the soil. Nutrients are tightly cycled by the rich soil. The vegetation is adapted to highly erratic precipitation patterns. The perennial groundcover prevents erosion and traps moisture. Furthermore, the whole system is well adapted to fire because the seeds of many prairie species require fire for germination. None of these features is maintained in conventional prairie agriculture, with its vast monocultures and dependence on fuel, fertilizer, and pesticides.

An agricultural mimic of the prairie can maintain many of the valuable functions of wild ecosystems while providing respectable crops of food, oils, and animal feed. As a form of agriculture uniquely suited to the land and climate, it works with the underlying ecological processes of the landscape. It replaces expensive and destructive external inputs with locally adapted intelligence.

An active landscape is neither completely "wild" nor excessively controlled in the manner of conventional water projects and agricultural systems. Like a good garden, it is a kind of conversation with nature. Ecological flood control, the Arcata marsh, and prairie-mimic agriculture hint at a landscape that "merges seamlessly with nature, yet is performing valuable services."[25] Such a landscape would draw us back into the circle of beings, meeting the needs of all species.

## SELF-DESIGN

Next to Stuart's desk is a tiny aquarium. This ecological microcosm, an old jar he filled with pond water a few weeks before, is full of surprises. A water hyacinth and a flourishing mat of duckweed and *Azolla* float on the surface. Underneath, the root hairs of the hyacinth constantly strain the water for nutrients, providing a home for various microorganisms. Decaying organic matter accumulates on the bottom, forming a kind of park for the playful water fleas and detritivores. Elsewhere, copepods swim in their characteristic herky-jerky fashion, tiny amphipods roil about, and snails slowly sweep the sides of the jar. Hundreds of species interact in this microcosm, their natural histories crisscrossing in a tiny world structured by roots, detritus, air, and water.

Other jars support very different ecosystems. In one jar, a green filigree of *Azolla* roots reaches all the way to the bottom. In another, flatworms graze the sides while hydras hold out their tentacles, seeking prey. In a third, a water hyacinth larger than the jar itself is bursting forth, transpiring water at four times the rate of any other system.

These modest microcosms are all seeded with the same pond water and plants, but they differ somewhat in their geometries and solar orientation. Over time, each microcosm transforms itself, producing a characteristic collection of species that makes effective use of the available sunlight and nutrients. The microcosms seem to grow more well adapted and interconnected.

There is a kind of *self-design* or *self-organization* at work here. Each microcosm spontaneously develops new levels of coherence and resilience that arise only from the rich interactions of the whole system. The flexibility of its component species allows it to respond to changing circumstances.

A simple experiment vividly illustrates the ability of systems to behave in ways far more complex than their individual parts. Begin by trapping a thin layer of water between two large plates, keeping the top and bottom plates at the same temperature. The water, as expected, remains completely homogenous. Start to slowly heat the bottom layer, producing a temperature difference between the plates. The water responds with a steady pattern of heat conduction from bottom to top (figure 15, left). When the temperature difference reaches a certain critical level, something remarkable happens. The water suddenly begins moving coherently, producing a series of convection cells or rolls (figure 15, right). The original conduction pattern becomes unstable. The system self-designs, enabling it to transport heat more effectively. The self-designing process operates without an overall plan: Local responses within the network of moving water molecules suddenly mesh together, producing coherent large-scale movements. A homogeneous pattern is replaced with a richly structured one.[26]

Another example is provided by the bizarre life-cycle of slime molds. They begin as free-living amoebas, absorbing nutrients in their vicinity. Over time, some of the cells grow hungry and emit a compound known as cAMP. Nearby cells follow the cAMP gradient toward the emitter, forming slow-moving waves. They gradually aggregate into a column of cells that begins to resemble a fungus. The cells at the top then transform themselves into a sporing appendage. The individual spores scatter in the wind, providing the starting cells for a new colony, and the whole cycle begins again. In a strange way, the slime molds are simultaneously a collection of free-living cells *and* multicellular cooperative entities. When triggered by a food shortage, the individual cells form coherent structures in a manner reminiscent of the convection cells.[27]

In our design practices, we have dealt very effectively with the entropic side of thermodynamics. We have designed engines and machines of every description and worked out their theoretical performance limits. But at the same time, we have largely neglected the *negentropic* side, in which systems maintain themselves far from equilibrium by using whatever flows of energy and materials are available. Once created, "the self-organized structure stays 'alive' by drawing nourishment from the surrounding flux and disorder. This is what happens when tornadoes and

FIGURE 15. *Demonstration of self-design in heating of water. Left: A steady pattern of heat conduction develops as heating proceeds. Right: Formation of Bénard convection cells at critical temperature differential.*

other cyclonic winds form out of turbulence. To keep themselves going, they feed off the thunderstorms, moisture, steep temperature and pressure gradients, and turbulence that gave them birth."[28] Jupiter's red spot is believed to function in this way. Indeed, all organisms flourish in a nonequilibrium state, feeding off freely available sunlight.

Self-designing systems like these present a rich possibility. If they are seeded with sufficient diversity, they can design their own solutions to the problems they are presented with. At first, this seems rather disconcerting. We are used to working out all the details. In highly complex situations, however, our limited knowledge may render such a level of control impossible. Letting go, trusting the capacities of a self-designing system, may be a better way of working constructively with complexity than attempting to oversimplify it.

Imagine a completely new kind of design partnership in which we catalyze the abilities of the right kind of system to self-design a solution. Just as the spaghetti-sauce-jar aquaria reconfigure themselves in response to their particular conditions, we may envision ecosystems that self-design to purify wastewater, provide food, or heal damaged landscapes. Such self-designing ecosystems have already found application in the new field of *ecological engineering*. Conventional engineering, notes Howard T. Odum, "replaces nature with new structure and process, but ecological engineering provides designs that use environmental structures and processes."[29] In other words, nature works for free. Using the self-designing tendencies of systems is always energetically cheaper than opposing them.

This approach asks us to acknowledge the inherent creativity of self-designing systems. It is this "capability of ecosystems that ecological engineering recognizes as a significant feature, because it allows nature to do some of the 'engineering.' We participate as the choice generator and as a facilitator of matching environments with ecosystems, but nature does the rest."[30] Self-designing systems respond well to a wide range of disturbances because they can strengthen whatever pathways are most valuable in a given situation, flexibly rearranging themselves to maintain their overall integrity.

The Ocean Arks International ecological wastewater treatment facility in Providence, Rhode Island, demonstrates the power and beauty of self-designing systems. It is located in a sleek greenhouse structure that stands in marked contrast to the grimy conventional treatment plant a hundred yards away. While the conventional plant relies on mechanical filtering, bacteria, and chemicals, the ecological system relies on the inherent capacity of aquatic ecosystems to purify water.

The greenhouse is filled to the brim with four rows of large, translucent cylinders that are overflowing with aquatic plants. Each row of cylinders is connected in a long series. It takes about four days for the water to flow from the first tank to the last tank. The earliest tanks contain the simple inhabitants of any nutrient-rich pond, including bacteria, algae, snails, and amphipods. Later tanks contain more delicate creatures: higher plants, clams, mollusks, and fish. Up top there is an inflow pipe labeled "SEWAGE," providing a gentle reminder that this delightful greenhouse is actually treating secondary effluent from Field's Point. Another sign, tongue-in-cheek, warns, "NO FISHING."

In effect, the greenhouse facility replicates the purification of water that occurs as it travels through a wetland. It contains a series of microcosms—tiny artificial ecosystems—that can support all the species necessary to take nutrients, pathogens, and toxins out of the water. As designer John Todd describes the process, "Microscopic bacteria consume the nutrient-laden organic matter from the wastewater and convert toxic ammonia to nitrite and nitrate, which creates suitable food for plants like duckweed. Algae growing on the sides of the tank consume abundant nutrients and grow rapidly. Snails and zooplankton feed on the algae. The zooplankton are then eaten by fish, such as striped bass, tilapia and minnows, etc.—and on and on churns the natural food chain cycle of an ecologically engineered system, purifying the wastewater with each step."[31]

In another part of the building are simulated tidal marshes, where the effluent passes through two distinct cycles: one without oxygen during high tide and one with oxygen during low tide. The marshes, which are planted with bulrushes, cattails, and other species, are an important source of metabolic diversity. As species diversity increases, so does the range of compounds that can be absorbed or neutralized.

This ecological wastewater treatment process is both beautiful and effective. The greenhouse environment is warm and inviting, the sound of trickling water permeates the building, and planter boxes hang from the ceiling. The system provides habitat for a wide range of species as an integral part of its functioning. By affirming the patterns that maintain healthy organisms and ecosystems, it achieves a high quality of treatment with minimal energy input and chemical intervention. The organisms themselves do the work of wastewater treatment, forming a kind of "living machine" much more flexible than its mechanical counterparts.

In conventional treatment, chlorine is added to sterilize the wastewater. While this meets the immediate goal of neutralizing pathogens with modest effectiveness, chlorine creates highly toxic byproducts. In a living machine, the diversity of plants, fish, and other species destroys pathogens in the hurly-burly of the rich tank environments. Clearly, a process that neutralizes toxins while producing clean water and supporting a verdant greenhouse is more desirable than a process that generates additional toxins and squanders nutrients.

The exquisite complexity of the Providence living machine was not fully orchestrated in advance. Instead, it unfolded as a threefold process embracing seeding with diversity, intelligence webs, and emergence. This threefold process underlies all successful self-designing systems. Seeding with diversity is a way of catalyzing creativity by providing a diverse repertoire of behaviors for the system to build on. Intelligence webs generate holistic responses from local perceptions and actions. Emergence is the spontaneous appearance of properties or levels of organization that are not apparent in the parts making up the system.

Self-designing systems perform valuable functions without explicit instructions. They grow their own connections, discover their own solutions, and create their own structures. They do all of this in a fully participatory way, without a central processing unit or a five-star general to coordinate the proceedings. Because new behaviors are allowed to emerge, self-designing systems confound our cherished notions of control, yet perform with grace and coherence.

Self-designing processes are more robust if they are seeded with a wide diversity of elements. Depending on the context, the diversity might be at the level of species, ecosystems, cultures, businesses, or technologies. The diversity allows adaptation to a great range of external disturbances and opportunities. For instance, polycultures help guarantee a minimal harvest since the crops will self-select under duress. Each element in a self-designing system is a source of knowledge, and therefore a possible contributor to a viable solution.

In a well-seeded system, the components can flourish even as they are challenged by changing conditions. They can maintain their integrity as individuals while entering a systemwide dialogue. Indeed, "once we understand the purposeful mechanisms built by natural selection we can recognize the splendid miniaturization and complexity [of ecosystems], which many misinterpreted earlier as a symptom of accident, disorder, and randomness. Guiding the self-managing systems of nature now seems far more sensible than the destruction of our life-support bases or dangerous, clumsy attempts to substitute our untried and expensive [technologies]."[32] The living world—in all its diversity—offers a rich source of evolutionary design wisdom, waiting to be tapped.

Seeding a living machine well is critical, since it relies on ecological diversity for self-repair, protection, and overall efficiency. In a statement of design principles for living machines, John Todd emphasizes many sorts of diversity: diverse microbial communities to provide a wide range of metabolic functions, diverse photosynthetic communities to utilize sunlight, diverse geological and mineral sources to provide trace nutrients, and diverse phyla, from bacteria to vertebrates, to explore all available niches. For sound thermodynamic reasons, "a diversity of organisms and habitats should permit the chemical [flexibility] of an ecologically engineered system to be maximized, since each phylum, taxon, and individual is characterized by unique biochemical signatures."[33] This flexibility is what allows the system to neutralize toxins and utilize a range of nutrients.

Todd also stresses the need for at least three different, strongly connected ecosystems in a living machine. This rule is very intriguing, for it hints that there is a threshold of complexity beyond which a system can self-design even under stress. Below this threshold, systems break down and deteriorate in novel situations. In the same way, there is a level of diversity beyond which agricultural systems become resistant to pests, diseases, and weeds, improve their nutrient cycling, and maintain their soil. Without this diversity, crops remain dependent on additional inputs for their continued survival.

The intelligence web is a self-designing system's behavioral core. It is a dance in which the elements of the system can resonate together, sharing information locally in a way that produces large-scale integrity. The intelligence web is not driven by a hierarchical chain of command. Instead, it grows and responds in a distributed fashion, without a center/periphery opposition. There is an unfolding of form and action that proceeds in strictly local fashion, yet produces systemwide harmonies.

The process of organismal growth and development, *morphogenesis,* provides a good example of an intelligence web. As trees grow, butterflies develop wing patterns, leopards form spots, or orchids bloom, a decentralized network of cells differentiates, splits, and shifts position, responding only to local signals. Just as convection cells create spatial structure from a featureless background when a critical temperature threshold is crossed, rich forms burst forth from the developing organism.

In a fire ant colony, notes Roger Lewin, "the nutritional needs of the colony are 'known' by the whole colony, because the workers constantly exchange samples of their stomach contents, effectively creating a single stomach for the colony."[34] In the same way, the organisms that work together in a living machine share a common chemical language. They collectively regulate their own metabolic processes and maintain conditions favorable for their own continuing existence. In an intelligence web, each element requires the others for its identity and context. There is information and intelligence not just in the pieces, but in the pattern of connections. Like a spider web, if it is touched in one place, it will respond in another.

The intelligence web is a counterpoint to the crisis of complexity discussed earlier. It is a decentralized response to complexity that allows local responses to be integrated through effective communication. For instance, cognitive scientists are finding that networks of neurons are able to store memories in a distributed fashion. No single neuron carries the memory, only a whole cluster of neurons acting in concert. The same is true of antibodies acting within the human immune system. Intelligence webs radically enhance the effectiveness of their components.

Emergence is at the heart of self-designing systems. Seed with diversity, let the intelligence web unfold, and the system may spontaneously exhibit rich new behaviors not possessed by its parts. Emergence is a leap to a qualitatively new level of self-integration. It is a new type of order bubbling up from the alchemy of rich interactions among simple components.

In the early seeding stages, a living machine is typically erratic. Sometimes it produces pure water, sometimes not. Yet it is beginning to self-design. Species are finding appropriate habitat, and their numbers are beginning to reflect the qualities of the incoming water. Suddenly, the system is able to handle wide variations in input while still producing reliably clean effluent. The system has acquired an emergent property: resilience.

Living machines are deliberately set up to self-design in response to the exact characteristics of the wastewater. In the Providence facility, "the sub-ecosystems self-design differently at each stage in response to input variations in external factors such as light or to internal variations in the strength of the waste stream. These self-design combinations are dynamic and highly varied."[35] It is rarely clear in advance what the key species will turn out to be; however, the initial seeding with a diversity of organisms, metabolisms, and habitats ensures that some viable system configuration will emerge.

If you place the common chemicals driving the Belousov-Zhabotinskii reaction in a petri dish, something rich and strange happens.[36] Contradicting our expectations of entropic decay and disorder, after a few minutes, spiral waves spread out in the dish (figure 16). Slight impurities anchor these emergent geometries, which are maintained by a series of reactions occurring far from equilibrium. This reaction is a good metaphor for self-designing systems. Through some unsuspected internal dynamic, they burst forth with a complexity and coherence all their own.

Instead of employing vast amounts of energy, materials, and

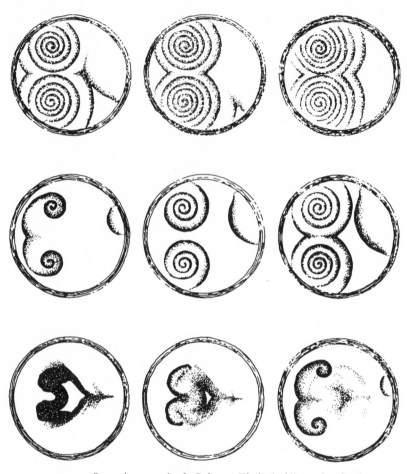

FIGURE 16. *Successive stages in the Belousov-Zhabotinskii reaction showing formation of spiral scroll waves*

centralized intelligence to control systems, it may be easier to encourage their own self-designing tendencies. We can allow useful properties to emerge rather than deliberately impose them. Self-design suggests a creative world, one of playful experimentation with new forms and possibilities. For too long we have expected the design professions to bend an inert world into shape. The alternative is to try to gently catalyze the self-designing potentialities of nature.

## ECOTONES

It is early morning on Richardson Bay, an arm of San Francisco Bay a few miles north of the Golden Gate Bridge. As Sim leaves his houseboat to row, the great blue heron perched on a piling next to the boat takes notice and shifts her weight uneasily. Sim goes about preparing his rowing shell, and she continues her vigil. A pair of egrets passes close by and takes up position on a nearby float. The gulls continue their noisy breakfast on the houseboat's roof, dropping mussel shells all about. As Sim glides along the water a few strokes from home, he notices a parallel wake close by. A sea lion raises his shiny black head for a moment, greets him with a short snort, and disappears into the cold grey waters.

He pulls past the old vessels, now improvised homes, which are anchored out beyond the dock, and heads out along the breakwater of the marina next door. The pilings are occupied by cormorants drying their outstretched wings and pelicans nestling long beaks on puffy chests. The morning air is still. A cottony layer of fog lies on the hills above Sausalito. The morning commute stream is heading up Waldo Grade toward the bridge. It is quiet on the waterfront except for the usual bantering of the gulls and the occasional screech of a passing egret. . . .

The edge of the bay is an example of what ecologists call an *ecotone*. It is an edge where two or more different types of natural environments join. Here their inhabitants come together to eat, mingle, reproduce, play, and enrich the game of life. An ecotone is a soft overlapping of very different regions. Like patches of watercolors on wet paper, different regions intermingle in an ecotone to create a new spectrum of colors. Ecotones are highly permeable. They are the opposite of a hard edge or boundary that presents a barrier to the flow of resources, energy, or communication. Not surprisingly, they also tend to be places of maximum biological diversity and productivity.

In its natural condition, the bay-edge ecotone where water meets land is usually a tidal marsh. In the marsh, freshwater meets saltwater, providing the proper salt content for the spawning and hatching of many species of marine life. The nutrients and detritus brought downstream are absorbed by bacteria living on aquatic grasses. They are, in turn, grazed by larger microscopic creatures that are food for small fish and frogs, themselves the prey of aquatic birds. An ecotone such as a marsh is an active, fecund place.

Along the shores of Richardson Bay, much of the native marsh ecotone is gone, although patches remain. The process began more than a hundred years ago, when unseaworthy ships were left to rot near the shoreline. Hills were blasted to make roads, and the rubble was dumped at the shore's edge. The native ecotone was damaged mostly by large-scale public projects: road building and war shipyards. If the planners of the 1940s had been given their way, an eight-lane highway would have been built along the waterfront, leaving only a dead zone between the highway and the water. Happily, this proposal was defeated. At the start of World War II, Kaiser and Bechtel—two large wartime contractors—built a huge new shipyard along several miles of the Sausalito waterfront on top of fill excavated during the construction of the new access highway to the Golden Gate Bridge. Along the shoreline road to the town of Mill Valley, more marsh was filled to make room for roadside businesses, and the road, which was underwater at high tides, was raised.

Unfortunately, most design is hostile to ecotones. In reaction to the rapid, haphazard growth of cities in the industrial era, city-planning practice as it developed in the early twentieth century zoned development into separate single-use land areas for housing, industry, commerce, and recreation. Government action discouraged and often ruthlessly eliminated the older, more organic concept of mixed uses in close proximity. Architects focused on creating new prototypes for single-use buildings. These templates inevitably neglected edges and interfaces with other systems.

Architects are still designing the *it,* and seldom the *edge,* even though it is at the edges, or ecotones, where the richest exchanges and interactions take place. The result is that modern cities and buildings have hard edges, and they tend to discourage ecotones. Planning and development still favor clear separation between land uses, and of course the automobile eats ecotones like a video-game Pac-Man. Thus we are left with the sterile empty plazas, parking lots, and highway edges of much new development.

The intentionally cultivated ecotone promotes contact among people and between people and nature. For example, the garden, the village, and the diversified family farm are historically rich ecotones that incorporate a complex set of interfaces between people and nature. Other ecotones are accidents. The town-gown edge where campuses meet the local community is an example. Here one finds the traditional habitat of intellectuals and bohemians, namely the coffeehouses and cheap eating places where theories are mulled over, politics dissected, and great and not-so-great ideas hatched. Grandiose urban-renewal schemes often sweep away such vibrant places.

While the native-marsh ecotone was being diminished by development, a new type of ecotone was being created along the Richardson Bay waterfront. The end of the war left the vast, once busy shipyards empty. Mountains of industrial and marine debris were abandoned. Serviceable vessels and machines could be had for next to nothing, and land and water space could be leased for a few dollars a month from the easy-going Portuguese who took over much of the former shipyards. A host of free-spirited folk began to recycle the junk left over from the dismantling of the war shipyards into impromptu aquatic homes. Steel landcraft, balloon barges, retired ferryboats replaced by the bridges, and industrial sheds became snug floating homes and workplaces. The waterfront attracted artists, writers, and intellectuals, including the philosopher Alan Watts and the artist Jean Varda, and small, creative, home-grown, useful ventures, like the first conceptual design/art group, Ant Farm, and Stewart Brand's *Whole Earth Catalog*. What had been a native ecotone of plants and animals became a remarkable social ecotone, an edge where a rich diversity of people and activities took hold, coexisting with the earlier native life.

By designing ecotones rather than hard edges, we intensify interactions. We bring together a greater diversity of life in an ecological ecotone, and we encourage greater cultural and economic diversity in an urban ecotone. In doing this, we facilitate the flows of materials, energy, and information that can catalyze self-designing processes.

### BIODIVERSITY

The biologist E. O. Wilson defines *biodiversity* as "the variety of organisms considered at all levels, from genetic variants belonging to the same species through arrays of species to arrays of genera, families, and still higher taxonomic levels; includes the variety of ecosystems, which comprise both the communities of organisms within particular habitats and the physical conditions under which they live."[37] Biodiversity is the true harvest of four billion years of evolutionary design. It is the pattern of connections that maintains life on this planet. Enfolded within biodiversity is the genetic information that fits organism to organism and organism to environment. The diversity of life encompasses some ten to fifty million species, each possessing from thousands to millions of genes. Our attempts to map this biological complexity are so incomplete that insect traps in the Amazon routinely catch dozens of completely new, uncatalogued species.

We're losing this diversity fast. Over evolutionary time, about one species per million has gone extinct each year. Human activity has increased this background level of extinction a thousandfold. According to Wilson, even the most cautious projections suggest that "the number of species doomed each year is 27,000. Each day it is 74, and each hour 3."[38] The diversity of life is a pharmacopoeia, a source of genetic variability for agriculture, a trove of potentially valuable materials. It is also much more than this. It is our evolutionary home.

Ecological design, at the deepest level, is design for biodiversity. If we fail to design with our fellow creatures in mind, we will ultimately fail ourselves. As the philosopher Bryan Norton suggests, "The value of biodiversity is the value of everything there is. It is the summed value of all the GNPs of all countries from now until the end of the world. We know that, because our very lives and our economies are dependent upon biodiversity."[39] Biodiversity is the most exquisite form of complexity in the world. It is holistic and dynamic, woven together within vast landscapes, in entire ecosystems, irreducible to species-by-species considerations. As we lose the Amazon rainforest, we lose clues to living well. Species that have made their way in the world suddenly lose their habitat and go extinct, forever extinguishing their coevolutionary wisdom.

A few years ago, a series of experiments focused on the effect of spatially complex environments on aphid–ladybird beetle interactions.[40] On plots with a continuous cover of goldenrod, the ladybird beetles kept aphid populations low through predation. On plots with a mixed pattern of goldenrod and grass patches, something surprising happened. The ladybird beetles were averse to moving over open grass, but the aphids were not. This enabled the aphids to disperse more quickly, finding temporary refuges from predation and increasing their numbers. Of course, with higher numbers of aphids, more beetles could also be supported. Adding spatial structure—changing the pattern of habitat—increased the population levels of both species.

We can take this story as a parable for the emerging view of ecology and complexity. The aphids and beetles do not reach a state of grace, some "balance of nature." They move back and forth on a landscape of grass and goldenrod, their numbers swelling here and declining there, with the ultimate outcome uncertain, hinging on random fluctuations. The historian Donald Worster echoes this theme: "Nature, many have begun to believe, is fundamentally erratic, discontinuous, and unpredictable. It is full of seemingly random events that elude our models of how things are supposed to work. As a result, the unexpected keeps hitting us in the face. Clouds collect and disperse, rain falls or doesn't fall, disregarding our careful weather predictions, and we cannot explain why."[41] The rich complexities of the natural world provide a powerful antidote to hubris, for if there are fundamental limits to our knowledge of ecosystem dynamics, we cannot easily "optimize" our tree farms, nature reserves, or levels of carbon dioxide emissions. We are left with humility and uncertainty.

Not so long ago, our ideas about the balance of nature promised the existence of mature communities with population levels at equilibrium. The theory of succession held that ecological communities moved through predictable stages to a final, climax community. A typical successional sequence might begin with bare rock colonized by sturdy organisms like mosses and lichens. Over time, the rock is broken down, slowly producing soil. This impoverished soil is suitable for a few tough grasses to take root. Later, taller plants provide shade and moderate the climate. After hundreds of years, a full-fledged forest develops. Other sequences for different climax ecosystems can easily be imagined.

While this story is undoubtedly roughly correct, there is growing evidence that the old picture of regular succession leading to a predictable climax community fails to capture many important nuances. One of the current controversies in ecology concerns the assembly of food webs—that is, how the various species making up an ecosystem actually come together. A recent computer simulation is revealing.[42] Several dozen species were randomly generated, filling roles as producers, consumers, and decomposers. Based on their roles, they were given propensities to cooperate or compete with one another. Artificial food webs were assembled by simulating the synthetic ecosystem, adding new species at random and deleting species as they went extinct. Remarkably, the assembled food webs were all different. There was no dominant set of species that could drive out the others, and therefore no climax community. Instead, the final outcome depended on the precise order in which species were added.

Biodiversity is not static. It is played out against a background of spatial complexity, disturbances, local extinctions, and landscape-level movements. Sometimes we prefer to imagine that biodiversity can still be supported by grossly oversimplified ecosystems, like the clearcut-riddled old-growth in the Pacific Northwest or a few wild but disconnected national parks or national wilderness areas. Sometimes, too, we forget that ecosystems have coevolved with characteristic types of disturbance— forests and prairies with wildfires, floodplains with floods—and that biodiversity hinges on complex patterns of habitat, climate, and renewal. It cannot be maintained one species at a time or in one place at a time. It depends on a whole continuum of landscapes, from the fully domesticated to the fully wild.

The problems connected with ecosystem stability are compounded when we recognize that populations are subject to various random influences, each tending to decrease their viability. Some of these influences, identified by R. Edward Grumbine, include:

1. *Genetic uncertainty,* or random changes in genetic makeup . . . which alter the survival and reproductive capabilities of individuals
2. *Demographic uncertainty* resulting from random events in the survival and reproduction of individuals in populations
3. *Environmental uncertainty* due to unpredictable changes in climate, weather, food supply, and the populations of competitors, predators, etc.
4. *Catastrophic uncertainty* from such phenomena as hurricanes, fires, droughts, etc., which occur at random intervals[43]

It is clear from this list that "ecologists are confronted with the question of why complex ecosystems do, in fact, exist."[44] The emerging answer is that local populations of a given species are continually going extinct, only to be reconstituted from nearby or more distant surviving populations. The whole landscape plays a role in keeping ecosystems intact. If we make ecosystems impervious to exchange, they fall apart. Ecosystems, even large ones, lack sufficient internal feedbacks to preserve themselves for very long. If "conservation biologists were pressed," observes Grumbine, "they might distill their theories into this advice: Think big, think connected, think whole."[45] In a deep sense, to maintain a single species, we must maintain certain critical aspects of the whole landscape, from the scale of a few miles to a few thousand miles. We must also maintain the communities that in turn support the species.

Diverse local ecosystems are the building blocks of biodiversity. However, the additional stability, resiliency, and self-designing properties they confer are contingent on the existence of other nearby ecosystems. Diverse ecosystems are healthy tiles in an ecological mosaic spanning entire continents. The ecological mosaic, in turn, can replenish its individual tiles when local disturbances or extinctions occur.

Biodiversity implies a diversity of species, but it also implies a diversity of ecosystems and, ultimately, of regions themselves. It can be preserved only by addressing all three levels: maintaining viable populations of native species, protecting representatives of all native ecosystem types in a range of successional states, and honoring wide-scale ecological processes including fire regimes, hydrological cycles, and movement patterns.[46] Such preservation in the face of critical threats like habitat fragmentation, road building, mining, destructive logging practices, and global climate change will require unprecedented kinds of ecological design.

Fortunately, the formative disciplines of landscape ecology and conservation biology are starting to give us some powerful design tools to maintain biodiversity even in the context of massive human interventions. The basic building block is a *core reserve* off-limits to all uses. Each reserve is bounded by a *buffer zone* with increasingly intensive land uses around it. An elaborate version of the reserve–buffer zone system has been adopted by UNESCO's Man and the Biosphere program, which has developed a global system of almost three hundred biosphere reserves.[47]

At the national level, the U.S. Fish and Wildlife Service is undertaking an ambitious biodiversity mapping project known as "gap analysis." This project works from layers of geographical vegetation data and known species-vegetation associations to identify unrepresented ecosystem types, habitats for endangered species, or diversity "hot spots." If these areas are unprotected, they are given priority status in the creation of future reserves or wilderness areas.[48]

But even carefully selected reserves are not sufficient to maintain biodiversity. Species that have suffered from severe habitat fragmentation may not be able to maintain viable populations without *wildlife corridors* (figure 17) to connect their small protected areas. Wildlife corridors increase effective habitat area by allowing safe movement across the landscape. Streambanks, power lines, and hedgerows are commonly occurring wildlife corridors, but they do not meet the needs of all species. Deliberately designed and protected corridors provide a crucial kind of *connectivity* in an otherwise fragmented landscape.[49]

Large mammals are particularly threatened by habitat loss. The grizzly bear offers the most disconcerting example. A single grizzly requires

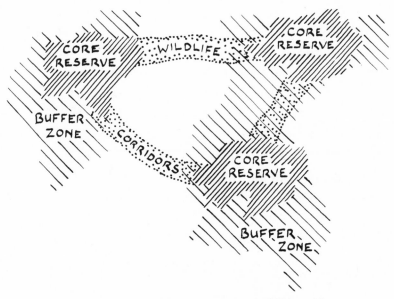

FIGURE 17. *Core reserves, buffer zones, and wildlife corridors*

about one hundred square miles for its home range. Given that five hundred or more bears are required for long-term population viability, this means a minimum of fifty thousand square miles of habitat, far larger than any wild area in the lower forty-eight states. Clearly, no single wilderness area will satisfy the grizzlies' habitat needs. However, wilderness corridors linking separate wilderness patches could potentially create an overall habitat area large enough to support a viable grizzly population. The following design guidelines, delineated by J. T. R. Kalkoven, show how this might work:

- Increase the size and the quality of the habitat patches in order to increase the local population size and to diminish the risk of extinction.
- Increase the number of patches in order to improve the possibility for [movement] and recolonization.
- Decrease the resistance of the landscape by including corridors and reducing the effect of barriers, in order to enhance the possibility of dispersal.[50]

These guidelines are being put to good use in the proposed Northern Rockies Ecosystem Protection Act (H.R. 2638). According to the supporting literature, "None of the remaining wildland ecosystems of the Wild Rockies Bioregion are of sufficient size to perpetuate self-sustaining populations of native wildlife and native biological diversity on their own—the ecosystems are dependent on each other. Therefore, a system of biological connecting corridors is protected by the Act. These wildland areas are found between the major ecosystems of the region and are essential for wildlife and plant migration and genetic interchange."[51] The act provides a holistic form of ecosystem protection that explicitly connects several of America's most beautiful wildernesses (figure 18) and is based on the principle that biodiversity thrives in interrelated ecosystems. Similar wilderness-corridor networks have been proposed for other areas, including the Cascade region straddling Washington State and British Columbia.

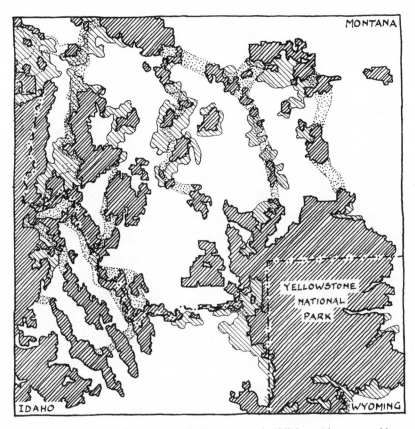

FIGURE 18. *System of core reserves, buffer zones, and wildlife corridors proposed by Northern Rockies Ecosystem Protection Act*

We are learning to see natural history in terms of unrepeatable yet patterned narratives that encompass the collected creature-wisdom of the planet. Classical economic notions of optimization and efficiency are no longer adequate to describe the ecological complexity surrounding us. As the ecologist Daniel Botkin has noted, "Wherever we seek to find constancy we discover change. . . . we find that [nature] is not constant in form, structure, or proportion, but changes at every scale of time and space. The old idea of a static landscape, like a single musical chord sounded forever, must be abandoned, for such a landscape never existed except in our imagination. Nature undisturbed by human influence seems more like a symphony whose harmonies arise from variation and change over every interval of time."[52] As we begin to see beyond cherished notions of equilibrium and balance in nature, we see a deeper, more exquisite set of patterns.

We must also recall that biological diversity and cultural diversity are deeply linked. Locally adapted traditional knowledge systems that help maintain diverse ecosystems are rapidly disappearing. "Diversity is the characteristic of nature and the basis of ecological stability," explains Vandana Shiva. "Diverse ecosystems give rise to diverse life forms, and to diverse cultures. The co-evolution of culture, life forms, and habitats has conserved the biological diversity on this planet. Cultural diversity and biological diversity go hand in hand."[53] Contemporary agribusiness and industry produce a kind of "monoculture of the mind," says Shiva. As ecosystems lose their diversity, so do our own patterns of thought. Designing for biodiversity will require us to break free of our monocultures of the mind and see clearly our embeddedness in the living world. The hard work, which is just beginning, is to translate this awareness into effective design strategies, at scales ranging from a backyard to a city to a continent.

## NOTES

1. Susan Oyama, "The Conceptualization of Nature: Nature as Design," in *Gaia 2: Emergence: The New Science of Becoming,* ed. William Irwin Thompson (Hudson, N.Y.: Lindisfarne Press, 1991), 180.

2. Thanks to Katy Langstaff for valuable discussions incorporated in this section.

3. This metaphor is from a lecture by Hardin Tibbs.

4. Ian McHarg, *Design with Nature* (Garden City, N.Y.: Natural History Press, 1969), 5.

5. Wendell Berry, *Collected Poems: 1957–1982* (San Francisco: North Point Press, 1984), 103.

6. Robert A. Frosch and Nicholas E. Gallopoulos, "Strategies for Manufacturing," *Scientific American* 261, no. 3 (September 1989): 144.

7. Lynn Margulis and Dorion Sagan, *Microcosmos: Four Billion Years of Microbial Evolution* (New York: Simon & Schuster, 1986), 99–114.

8. Hardin Tibbs, "Industrial Ecology: An Environmental Agenda for Industry," *Whole Earth Review*, no. 77 (winter 1992): 9.

9. Yan Jingsong and Ma Shijun, "The Function of Ecological Engineering in Environmental Conservation with Some Case Studies from China," in *Ecological Engineering for Wastewater Treatment*, ed. Carl Etnier and Björn Gutterstam (Gothenburg, Sweden: Bokskogen, 1991), 89.

10. Barbara Matilsky, *Fragile Ecologies: Contemporary Artists' Interpretations and Solutions* (New York: Rizzoli, 1992), 111.

11. John Harte et al., *Toxics A to Z: A Guide to Everyday Pollution Hazards* (Berkeley and Los Angeles: Univ. of California Press, 1991), 54.

12. This work is being pioneered by the Gaia Institute in New York City.

13. California Waste Exchange, *Directory of Industrial Recyclers and Listing of Hazardous Wastes Available for Recycling* (Sacramento: Department of Toxic Substances Control, Hazardous Waste Management Program, 1993).

14. Tibbs, *Industrial Ecology*, 5.

15. Ibid., 9–10.

16. John Tillman Lyle, *Design for Human Ecosystems: Landscape, Land Use, and Natural Resources* (New York: Van Nostrand Reinhold, 1985), 236–7.

17. Ann L. Riley, "The Greening of Federal Flood Control Policies: The Wildcat–San Pablo Creeks Case," in *The Ecological City: Preserving and Restoring Urban Biodiversity*, ed. Rutherford H. Platt, Rowan A. Rowntree, and Pamela C. Muick (Amherst: Univ. of Massachusetts Press, 1994), 217–30.

18. G. Hollis et al., "Wise Use of Resources," *Nature and Resources* 24 (1988): 2–13.

19. John Tillman Lyle, *Regenerative Design for Sustainable Development* (New York: John Wiley & Sons, 1994), 102.

20. Michael Hough, "Design with City Nature," in *The Ecological City: Preserving and Restoring Urban Biodiversity*, ed. Rutherford H. Platt, Rowan A. Rowntree, and Pamela C. Muick (Amherst: Univ. of Massachusetts Press, 1994), 44.

21. Robert L. Thayer, Jr., *Gray World, Green Heart: Technology, Nature, and the Sustainable Landscape* (New York: John Wiley & Sons, 1994), 263.

22. For information on the Arcata marsh, see Lyle, *Regenerative Design*, 242–3; Thayer, *Gray World*, 155–9; and Doug Stewart, "Nothing Goes to Waste in Arcata's Teeming Marshes," *Smithsonian* 21, no. 1 (April 1990): 175–9.

23. Ibid., 177.

24. Judith D. Soule and Jon K. Piper, *Farming in Nature's Image: An Ecological Approach to Agriculture* (Washington, D.C.: Island Press, 1992), 133–4.

25. David Austin, personal communication.

26. For a detailed explanation of this phenomenon, known as the Bénard convection, see Gregoire Nicolis and Ilya Prigogine, *Exploring Complexity: An Introduction* (New York: W. H. Freeman, 1989), 8–13.

27. The odd dynamics of slime molds are discussed in Arthur T. Winfree, *When Time Breaks Down: The Three-Dimensional Dynamics of Electrochemical Waves and Cardiac Arrhythmias* (Princeton: Princeton Univ. Press, 1987), 173–7.

28. John Briggs, *Fractals: The Patterns of Chaos: Discovering a New Aesthetic of Art, Science, and Nature* (New York: Simon & Schuster, 1992), 112.

29. Howard T. Odum, "Ecological Engineering and Self-Organization," in *Ecological Engineering: An Introduction to Ecotechnology,* ed. William J. Mitsch and S. E. Jørgensen (New York: John Wiley & Sons, 1989), 80.

30. William J. Mitsch and S. E. Jørgensen, "Introduction to Ecological Engineering," in *Ecological Engineering: An Introduction to Ecotechnology,* ed. William J. Mitsch and S. E. Jørgensen (New York: John Wiley & Sons, 1989), 6.

31. Tom Crane and John Todd, "Solar Aquatics: Nature's Engineering," *Pollution Engineering* (15 May 1992): 51.

32. Howard T. Odum, *Environment, Power, and Society* (New York: John Wiley & Sons, 1971), 101.

33. This quotation is from a manuscript version of Paul Mankiewicz's paper "Biological Surfaces, Metabolic Capacitance, Growth, and Differentiation: A Theoretical Exploration of Thermodynamic, Economic, and Material Efficiencies in Fluid Purification Systems," a 1993 report from the Center for Restoration of Waters, Falmouth, Mass.

34. Roger Lewin, *Complexity: Life at the Edge of Chaos* (New York: Macmillan, 1992), 175.

35. John Todd, "Living Machines for Pure Water: Sewage as Resource," in *Mending the Earth: A World for Our Grandchildren,* ed. Paul Rothkrug and Robert L. Olson (Berkeley: North Atlantic Books, 1991), 117–8.

36. See Nicolis and Prigogine, *Exploring Complexity,* 15–26.

37. Edward O. Wilson, *The Diversity of Life* (Cambridge: Harvard Univ. Press, 1992), 393.

38. Ibid., 280.

39. Bryan Norton, "Commodity, Amenity, and Morality: The Limits of Quantification in Valuing Biodiversity," in *Biodiversity,* ed. Edward O. Wilson (Washington, D.C.: National Academy Press, 1988), 201.

40. These experiments are discussed in P. Karieva, "Predator-Prey Dynamics in Spatially Structured Populations: Manipulating Dispersal in a Coccinellid-Aphid Interaction," *Mathematical Ecology: Lecture Notes in Biomathematics* 54 (Berlin: Springer-Verlag, 1984), 368–89.

41. Donald Worster, "The Ecology of Chaos and Harmony," *Environmental History Review* 14 (1990): 13.

42. See, for instance, J. A. Drake, "The Mechanics of Community Assembly and Succession," *Journal of Theoretical Biology* 147 (1990): 213–34.

43. R. Edward Grumbine, *Ghost Bears: Exploring the Biodiversity Crisis* (Washington, D.C.: Island Press, 1992), 32.

44. D. L. DeAngelis and J. C. Waterhouse, "Equilibrium and Nonequilibrium Concepts in Ecological Models," *Ecological Monographs* 57, no. 1 (1987): 1–21.

45. Grumbine, *Ghost Bears*, 62.

46. Reed F. Noss and Allen Y. Cooperrider, *Saving Nature's Legacy: Protecting and Restoring Biodiversity* (Washington, D.C.: Island Press, 1994), 89.

47. For a rich, extended discussion of biosphere reserves, see *The Law of the Mother: Protecting Indigenous People in Protected Areas,* ed. Elizabeth Kemf (San Francisco: Sierra Club Books, 1993).

48. Noss and Cooperrider, *Saving Nature's Legacy*, 113–8.

49. Ibid., 150–7.

50. J. T. R. Kalkoven, "Survival of Populations and the Scale of the Fragmented, Agricultural Landscape," in *Landscape Ecology and Agroecosystems,* ed. R. G. H. Bunce et al. (Boca Raton, Fla.: Lewis Publishers, 1993), 89.

51. *Northern Rockies Ecosystem Protection Act* (Missoula, Mont.: Wild Rockies Action Fund, 1993). Pamphlet.

52. Daniel B. Botkin, *Discordant Harmonies: A New Ecology for the Twenty-First Century* (New York: Oxford Univ. Press, 1990), 62.

53. Vandana Shiva, *Monocultures of the Mind: Perspectives on Biodiversity and Biotechnology* (London: Zed Books, 1993), 65.

## FOURTH PRINCIPLE

# EVERYONE IS
# A DESIGNER

*Listen to every voice in the design process. No one is
participant only or designer only: Everyone is a
participant-designer. Honor the special knowledge
that each person brings. As people work together to
heal their places, they also heal themselves.*

### CULTIVATING DESIGN INTELLIGENCE

We are all designers. We constantly make decisions that shape our own futures and those of others. We choose our everyday reality: where and how we live, how we use our time and energy, what we value and whom we care about, how we earn and how we spend. All these choices involve dimensions of design.

For most of our tenure as a species, design has been intuitive. It has been embedded in culture, learned through daily participation in the life of the family and community. Local knowledge and materials gave communities everything necessary to design, build, and maintain their places. Every community member knew the appropriate design templates and could replicate most of them. Everyone could build a wall that would stand up, lay out a rice terrace impervious to erosion, or construct a cooking fireplace that concentrated the heat under the pot. People lived with their designs, directly—sometimes painfully—experiencing success or failure, and learning accordingly. People learned to be designers by doing.

More recently, a vast professional design apparatus has supplanted these intuitive design processes. In the United States, few people have the competence to build their own houses, grow their own food, or provide their own water—tasks once considered fundamental to any community member. Dozens of fragmented design disciplines shape the material basis of our lives. As a consequence, the ecological implications of design have largely been removed from our awareness.

Ecological design suggests a deeply participatory process in which technical disciplinary languages and barriers are exchanged for a shared understanding of the design problem. Ecological design changes the old rules about what counts for knowledge and who counts as knower. It suggests that sustainability is a cultural process rather than an expert one, and that we should all acquire a basic competence in the shaping of our world.

Unfortunately, in the case of architecture, conventional educational practices still largely follow the myth put forward by Ayn Rand in her novel *The Fountainhead,* in which a lone idiosyncratic architect fights against a hostile and philistine world. Architectural design is generally not taught as a collaborative process that clients or users have any stake in. Rather, it is often taught as a "pure" process that should not be "contaminated" by any real-world constraints or needs: social, environmental, or economic. It is even fashionable to approach design education as a form of personal therapy—the artist's struggle for self-expression.

Architecture was still a craft at the time of the *atelier,* the studio apprentice system that developed at École des Beaux-Arts in Paris during the nineteenth century. Students apprenticed to working architects, who also gave them design exercises. Architects were concerned with form and style, which tended to follow Greek, Roman, Gothic, and Renaissance precedents. Students learned these styles by constructing painstaking pencil and watercolor drawings of admired examples from the past. The studio master would concoct programs or briefs for imaginary building projects that the students would design. Their individually produced works were judged at reviews by panels of architects, and prizes were awarded for the most outstanding designs.

The studio system was gradually incorporated within university education in the United States and other countries, beginning with the first university-level professional training in architecture at the Massachusetts Institute of Technology in 1868. Almost unchanged, it is still the dominant force in design education today. If you visit any one of the roughly one hundred collegiate schools of architecture and design in the United States, you will find a special world removed from the rest of university life. Architecture students typically spend long nights, weekends, and much of their class time laboring over drafting tables in studios cluttered with pinned-up drawings, half-finished models, and wastebaskets overflowing with crumpled-up yellow tracing paper.

For better or worse, the culture of design grows out of the studio system. To their credit, studios do offer unique opportunities for interdisciplinary learning and wide synthesis. They provide large blocks of time to examine problems in depth. Students learn through case studies, although these are rarely grounded in actual places and communities. In fact, the studio could provide an important venue for teaching ecological design. It could be a place where students are introduced to real problems and real people, a place of rich interaction with other disciplines both inside and outside the university. It could allow students to learn design as a cooperative, interdisciplinary activity.

Stewart Brand, creator of the *Whole Earth Catalog* and an astute observer of architects and building, suggests that the problem with architectural design education is that the real players and the real information are kept out of the learning:

> By considering buildings whole, university architecture departments could reverse their trend towards senescence. They could invigorate the faculty with an infusion of facilities managers, preservationists, interior designers, developers, project managers, engineers, contractors, construction lawyers, and insurance mongers. The department could promote some of the marginalized people they already have—building economists, vernacular building historians, and post occupancy evaluators. In that enriched context, what's left of art oriented architecture would have all that its creativity could handle exploring new syntheses of the flood of data and ideas.[1]

Studios as research/design clinics could begin to build a cumulative knowledge base that is lacking in design fields such as architecture. The present work of design studios is wasted on one-time exercises that are rarely implemented outside the classroom. Studios based on analyzing particular issues—megacities, urban wildlife corridors, the future of suburbs, constructed wetlands—would provide a continuous cycle of information. Instead of "seeing our education as a training in the design of buildings," writes Thomas Fisher, "some are beginning to see that what we really learn is how to assimilate large amounts of disparate information and find ways to order it and apply it to different settings."[2]

Only through actually implementing a design does one begin to understand it. Since design students never actually implement their designs and are often separated from real-world concerns, they are starved for concrete experience. In other professions, including law and medicine, supervised fieldwork is part of the education. In these professions, academic theory and actual practice reinforce and complement each other. Fieldwork is a way of focusing attention on issues that deserve more attention. In fact, much of the pioneering work on ecological design began as field-oriented classes through established design schools and nonprofit education and research centers such as the Farallones Institute and the New Alchemy Institute.

Donald Watson, a leader in sustainable design, suggests a number of immediate opportunities for cooperation among the schools and the professions:

- Case studies and postoccupancy appraisals of buildings. Using simple evaluation tools, teams could carry out case-study evaluations of how particular environments and buildings actually perform.
- Design competitions. Design competitions stimulate public and professional awareness of new ideas. In California, a competition to design new energy-efficient state buildings worked to educate architects and was used as a studio project. Three student/faculty teams were among the top winners.
- Community workshops. Community design workshops—sometimes called *charettes*—are an effective way to involve the public in community design issues and enhance their understanding of new strategies.[3]

Another possibility is to create a new ecological design discipline within existing academic institutions. An ecological design center on campus would explicitly address the massive social and environmental crisis we face. Through practical design projects, students would learn to work with wider communities and acquire basic ecological literacy, thereby gaining the valuable habit of responding effectively to complex, interdisciplinary problems in their own backyards. David W. Orr provides a list of typical projects such a center could undertake:

- Design of a building with no outside energy sources that recycles all waste generated by occupants, constructed from locally available, environmentally benign materials
- Development of a bioregional directory of building materials
- Inventory of campus resource flows

- Restoration of a degraded ecosystem on or near campus
- Design of a low-input, sustainable farm system
- Economic survey of resource and dollar flows in the regional economy
- Design of living machines for campus effluents[4]

We are accustomed to seeing designers as artists or technicians, each role insulated in its own way from everyday life. Architect Linda Groat proposes a third possibility more germane to ecological design: the designer as cultivator.

> The term *cultivator* derives from the same Latin root as the word *culture*. . . . The contemporary sense of the word includes not only the nurturing of the land, but also the care and training of the human mind and sensibilities. . . . Whereas the architect-as-artist stands apart from or in opposition to society, the cultivator is fully engaged . . . whereas the architect-as-technician responds to the power and autonomy of social and physical forces, the cultivator possesses a "personal perspective" animated by transpersonal interaction and "motivated to express and embody in living acts and artifacts a humanized, cosmically rooted intelligence."[5]

In this vivid image, designers consciously cultivate a shared ground for ecological design intelligence. *Design* is from the Latin *de signare,* which means "to trace out, define, indicate." Too often, this tracing, defining, and indicating has been for the purpose of *exclusion* rather than *inclusion*. Ecological design, by infusing design itself with the common life around us, calls us back to an inclusive circle in which all voices are once again heard.

## COMMUNITY DESIGN

As we have seen, cultivating design intelligence requires that design education once again become permeable to the outside world, responding to

the challenges offered by real places and adding ecology and community
to its list of concerns. It also requires a recognition that design is far too
important to be left solely to designers. Design is not neutral. It is
molded by powerful political and economic forces. It is well past time to
open up the methods, products, and apparatus of design to wider
constituencies.

Ecological design literacy provides a basic foundation for shaping design decisions at all levels of scale: Should the town invest in an expensive
conventional sewage treatment plant, or should it consider a constructed
wetland? What kind of lumber should I use for my house? What sort of
urban-growth policy should the city seek? These are questions that professionals have an important role in deciding, but the final choice rests on
a decision-making process that takes into account the wider cultural and
ecological context of each solution.

At the community scale, ecological design is an experiment in democ-
racy. Daniel Kemmis, mayor of Missoula, Montana, writes of an issue
that divided his town a few years ago. Missoula, located in a broad mountain valley, is often subject to inversion layers during the winter. These
layers were trapping the smoke from thousands of wood stoves, producing unacceptable levels of particulates. In this case, a renewable local
resource—wood—was causing damage to the shared airshed. Some citizens wanted to ban wood burning; others, viewing the issue as one of individual rights, said something to the effect of "You mean you're going to
tell me now that I can't go into the forest and cut my own wood and take
it home and burn it in my own living-room fireplace?"[6]

As it turned out, the town opted to allow wood burning, but in a new
way. Local regulations have spurred the creation of several enterprises
"which are profitably engaged in manufacturing clean-burning stoves, or
compressed wood pellets to burn cleanly in them, or furnace accessories
to enable commercial or institutional customers to burn those pellets."[7]
In this community design process, everyone has learned more about pollution, managing a common airshed, and the intricacies of wood stoves.

More important, the community has learned to communicate and cooperate, setting a precedent for further efforts.

William Morrish, director of the Design Center for American Urban Landscape at the University of Minnesota, has worked with many local communities on issues of flood prevention, urban redevelopment, and ecological restoration. He leads tours with local citizens during which everyone—professional or not—takes photographs and makes notes. He has invariably found the comments of the townsfolk to be rich with local knowledge and therefore of great value in the design process.[8]

Since environmental impacts are rarely confined to an individual, the reduction of such impacts typically requires that a commons be reclaimed or created afresh. In the case of Missoula, the seemingly private issue of burning wood in one's stove turned out to have large-scale effects that could be mitigated only by working within an airshed commons. In other cases, a watershed, a marsh, or a whale's migratory path might constitute the relevant commons.

From the fugue of local voices within a commons will emerge stories of survival and renewal, clues to designs that will make sense in the context of the whole community. Since ecological designs typically unfold over many years or decades, it is imperative that they coevolve with the wishes of their future stewards. It is impossible to simply walk away from a living system as one would walk away from a freshly built skyscraper or house. The sheer complexity and subtlety of ecological design requires scrupulous attendance to direct experiences of place.

The kind of integrative thinking and action required for effective ecological design is widespread among people of all ages. At the San Domenico School in San Anselmo, California, the Ecological Design Institute is working to implement an ecological design curriculum for prekindergarten through twelfth grade. The curriculum emphasizes hands-on problem solving that transcends conventional boundaries. Katy Langstaff, the project coordinator, writes that "young people today are inheriting a world of complexity beyond what a compartmentalized curriculum can train them for. Careers of tomorrow will require holistic thinking, problem solving, and ethics."[9] Working with the students at three levels of scale—watershed, campus, and on-site garden—the project is attempting to foster an awareness of place and an appreciation for the significance of design.

At Intermediate School 167 in the Bronx, children are being given the opportunity to learn biology, ecology, and chemistry through a hands-on restoration project, reclaiming a small patch of meadow and wetland fronting the Bronx River and adjacent to the school. This engagement with their own place provides wonderful training in ecological design. As one of the teachers recalls:

> Each session was a continual flow of excitement and energy, stemming from the curiosity of so many engaged, young minds. Planting, mulching, and watering became an adventure. Through activity and observation, many questions were raised. Students quickly learned about the correspondence between the river, the insects, snakes, snails and turtle eggs we found, and the sandy, loamy banks and the herbs, shrubs, and trees we planted.
>
> Our project also helped develop leadership and communication skills among the sixth graders from various ethnic backgrounds. A few were knowledgeable in horticultural techniques from agricultural experiences in their native countries. An effort which combined landscape restoration, past history, and transplanted cultures began to take root here in the new world of the south Bronx.[10]

These examples show that everyone can participate in the design process. Such participation, with its rich tangle of theoretical knowledge, manual skills, and communication, is at the core of a culture of sustainability.

Another powerful way of opening up the design process is to establish a set of indicators to which a community can easily respond. Just as a dry reservoir provides direct and incontrovertible information about water storage, or a fundraising thermometer at a building site tells us how the project is progressing, we might imagine prominent meters displayed near City Hall that showed current levels of energy or water use. Well-chosen indicators can help form a shared awareness of the issues facing a community. They can give us a way of evaluating our own activities and understanding their wider implications. Just as *indicator species* like salmon mark the health of ecosystems, indicators for sustainability report on the health of human communities.

According to Sustainable Seattle, a grassroots project developing environmental indicators, good indicators share the following four features: They are "bellwether tests of sustainability, can be understood and accepted by the community, have interest and appeal for use by local media, and are statistically measurable."[11] The project has identified forty indicators for a sustainable Seattle and is in the process of carefully documenting each one with descriptions, definitions, interpretations, evaluations, linkages to other indicators, and a graphical display of trends. As one project report stated, "While these indicators have not been derived from a scientifically tested and refined model of sustainability (for such models are not to be found), neither are they arbitrary, having evolved through dialogue with people of knowledge and insight."[12] The indicators are to be taken as a rough cut at the problem of making sustainability tangible in a city facing enormous environmental pressures. The following selection of ten of the project's indicators gives a taste of the process. Indicators moving toward sustainability are marked +, and those moving away are marked –.

*Environment*
Wild salmon runs through local streams –
Percentage of Seattle streets meeting "Pedestrian-Friendly" criteria +

*Population and Resources*
Total population of King County –
Tons of solid waste generated and recycled per capita per year –

*Economy*

Percentage of employment concentrated in the top ten employers +

Percentage of children living in poverty –

Percentage of citizenry that can afford adequate housing –

*Culture and Society*

Juvenile crime rate –

Percentage of youth participating in a form of community service +

Participation in the arts +


The Sustainable Seattle indicators ground sustainability in the particular problems and opportunities facing the city, helping ordinary citizens become involved in complex decision-making processes that were once the exclusive domain of city planners, solid-waste commissioners, economists, and other professionals. The city is currently providing a full-time neighborhood planner to each neighboorhood in the city, and the indicators are playing an important role in local planning processes.

The notion of community sustainability indicators can be easily extended to community sustainability planning. It is often useful to begin the planning process with a series of *charettes,* or intensive design workshops, that bring community members together with those possessing professional design expertise. In charettes, participants are instructed to label and illustrate cards with facts (What?), goals (Why?), or solutions (How?). Facts provide detailed information about the community: for example, "Fox Creek is flooding one year out of three." Goals represent important aspirations: "The downtown core should be revitalized." Solutions are possible design interventions: "Create a new kind of agricultural zoning to protect farms threatened by development." When the cards are pinned to the wall, the group can begin to identify important clusters and patterns, rearranging the cards as necessary. The card wall provides a changeable map, a consensus of people's beliefs, perceptions, and ideas about a shared problem. It works best when it can be placed in an accessible space where it can be reviewed, commented on, and added to.

Other methods are just as effective. People can be asked to draw maps of the community, labeling places of particular cultural, ecological, or economic interest. Layers of geographical information on vegetation, geology, hydrology, soils, roads, land use, property lines, and so forth can be printed on acetate sheets. Participants can then color, overlay, and label these sheets to create idiosyncratic maps. Computerized geographical information systems (GIS) can even be used to perform this work more precisely and create highly sophisticated maps for wider circulation. For instance, reports Doug Aberley, the Nisga'a people of northwestern British Columbia have recently purchased "state of the art G.I.S. computer software and are now digitizing satellite images of their territory to defend sovereignty, and aid in the stewardship of locally controlled forests, fisheries, and other resources."[13] An exciting recent issue of *Cultural Survival Quarterly* discusses other mapping efforts conducted by indigenous people around the world.[14]

This local knowledge can be combined with some basic ecological accounting to provide a detailed inventory of place rich enough to answer questions like these:

- What are the prevalent soil types? How healthy is the soil in this region?
- Are there any endangered species in the region?
- Is there any evidence of deleterious health effects from local industry?
- How much gasoline, natural gas, electricity, solar energy, and fuelwood are used?
- How much food is produced locally? What types? How much of this food is actually used locally?
- How much money is spent in the community? How much leaves the community?
- Are there any underutilized wastes?

Meaningful indicators or specific goals emerge from this inventory and from the charette process itself. If the community is excessively dependent on oil for its winter heating needs, it may take as a goal a certain level of reduction in this use. If the community is facing serious health risks from toxic chemicals, it may address this issue first. Community sustainability planning is an incremental process. It brings the community to a gradually increased awareness of the flows of energy, materials, money, and information that maintain a place. It can work only with the active involvement of a broad range of stakeholders, from schoolchildren to businesspeople to artists.

In the community sustainability planning process, everyone is a designer. Everyone makes decisions about transportation, buildings, water, energy, food, and waste. Since these design decisions have deep implications for the health of the entire community, they are best made in a widely participatory way. This is not to suggest that everyone can become a master builder or a competent ecological engineer. However, we can all possess a basic design literacy that allows us to participate in the shaping of our places.

Ecological design cuts through the insularity of the various design professions. The work of making our communities and regions sustainable provides a rich curriculum for all who would undertake it. As Wes Jackson says, this work provides a major in "Homecoming." It is nitty-gritty work, not necessarily glamorous, but too important to the real life of communities to be left to professional designers and other experts.

NOTES

1. Stewart Brand, *How Buildings Learn: What Happens After They're Built* (New York: Viking, 1994), 215.

2. Thomas Fisher, "Can This Profession Be Saved?" *Progressive Architecture* 75, no. 2 (February 1994): 84.

3. Donald Watson, "Agenda 2000: A Proposal for Leadership by the Design Professions," *Symposium on Sustainable Strategies for Communities and Building Materials.* Paper presented at conference of American Institute of Architects, Seattle, October 1993. For information on post-occupancy, see Sim Van der Ryn and Murray Silverstein, *Dorms at Berkeley: An Environmental Analysis* (Berkeley: Univ. of California, Center for Planning and De-

velopment Research, 1967). The competition for an energy-efficient office building was sponsored by the Office of the State Architect.

4. David W. Orr, *Earth in Mind* (Washington, D.C.: Island Press, 1994), 110–11. See also the discussion in Herman E. Daly and John B. Cobb, Jr., *For the Common Good: Redirecting the Economy Toward Community, the Environment, and a Sustainable Future* (Boston: Beacon Press, 1989), 357–60.

5. Linda Groat, "Architecture's Resistance to Diversity: A Matter of Theory as Much as Practice," *Journal of Architectural Education* 47, no. 1 (September 1993): 8–9.

6. Daniel Kemmis, *Community and the Politics of Place* (Norman: Univ. of Oklahoma Press, 1990), 90.

7. Ibid., 91–2.

8. See the publications of the Design Center for the American Urban Landscape, College of Architecture and Landscape Architecture, Univ. of Minnesota.

9. Katy Langstaff, from a report for the Sustainable San Domenico Project, The Ecological Design Institute, 1994.

10. Diana Hernandez, "Restoration through Education/Education through Restoration," *Restoration and Management Notes* 10, no. 1 (summer 1992): 16.

11. Pamphlet from the Sustainable Seattle Indicators Project, 1993.

12. Ibid.

13. Doug Aberley, "Eye Memory: The Inspiration of Aboriginal Mapping," in *Boundaries of Home: Mapping for Local Empowerment,* ed. Doug Aberley (Gabriola Island, British Columbia: New Society Publishers, 1993), 15. This book is a highly recommended introduction to the process of community mapping.

14. "Geomatics: Who Needs It?" *Cultural Survival Quarterly* 18, no. 4 (winter 1995).

# MAKE NATURE VISIBLE

*De-natured environments ignore our need and our*
*potential for learning. Making natural cycles and*
*processes visible brings the designed environment*
*back to life. Effective design helps inform us of our*
*place within nature.*

Sim used to surprise his architecture students with a special test. Not about styles, building codes, or drafting techniques, the test was about an awareness of processes in one's home place. Simple questions: How does the water you drink reach your kitchen sink? How many days until the moon is full? What soil series are you standing on? From what direction do winter storms generally come in your region?[1] The same students who routinely displayed a sophisticated knowledge of current architectural theory or computer-aided design were overwhelmed by the test. It called for a different sort of knowledge. In the end, few students answered more than three out of ten right.

Our environments—whether they are sprawling malls or wild rivers— are the most powerful teachers we have. In a de-natured place, we are likely to develop de-natured imaginations, lacking room for Bishop pines or upswimming salmon. Robin Grossinger notes that in the span of one century "we've not only destroyed the original landscape, but we've very nearly lost the collective ability to remember what it looked like before."[2] We have culverted the creeks, paved the wetlands, and built on the farms, orchards, and meadows that once nourished young minds. We have rendered both nature and the consequences of our own technologies increasingly invisible.

Dumb design has set a complex epistemological trap for us. Many of us live in cities where both ecological and technological processes are hidden from our everyday awareness. The designed environment does not reveal to us how technology supports us and how in turn it is interconnected with the natural world. Our working days are spent in modern buildings that are sealed from the elements. Often we can't even open the windows. Their design gives us few clues regarding orientation, climate, the sun's position, or seasonal change. The pipes and cables that bring in fuel, electricity, and water are hidden from view. During the night, food arrives and garbage is collected, all out of sight. We don't see the many tons of carbon dioxide that pour out of a typical car each year. We don't taste the toxic cocktails in our food or water.

What do we learn from this kind of "nowhere" environment? When living and working in nowhere places becomes normal, it is no wonder that we literally lose some of our sensitivity toward nature. Through the daily experience of the designed environment, we learn detachment. There are few designed-in opportunities that encourage us to care for the environment around us.

There is a pernicious cycle at work here. As our systems of food, water, energy, waste, and sewage have grown ever more intricate and hidden, it has become more difficult to understand or question them. As nature has receded from our daily lives, it has receded from our ethics.

Now we are beginning the slow work of turning this destructive cycle into a regenerative one. By making nature visible again, favoring

technologies that are not hidden and that do not possess hidden consequences, our imaginations are again enfolded in nature. We hunger for
the channelized creek to return to its wooded, meandering banks; we are
no longer content to buy toxic products; we act in new ways.

Design transforms awareness. Designs that grow out of and celebrate
place ground us in place. Designs that work in partnership with nature
articulate an implicit hope that we might do the same. Designs that call
for our continuing participation and involvement offer us new teachings
day by day. Ecological design brings us back to the wider living community, waking us again to the patterns of wind and rain, the sources of our
food, and the life-cycles of our materials. It illuminates the very flows that
sustain us. Such learning is the most important of all.

If the built environment is a powerful silent teacher, we can change the
message people get from it. It can be redesigned so that people are richly
informed about their place and the ecological processes endemic to it. In
the Bateson Building, for example, Sim and his colleagues found that by
designing with natural energy flows, they became sensitive to rhythms of
light and climate. We are not adapted to live or work at temperatures or
lighting levels that are uniform and constant; we are most alive when we
experience subtle cycles of difference in our surroundings. By this logic,
a building should itself become in Gregory Bateson's words, a "pattern
that connects" us to the change and flow of climate, season, sun, and
shadow, constantly tuning our awareness of the natural cycles that support all life. A wall should be not a static, two-dimensional architectural
element but a living skin that adapts to differences in temperature and
light. Designing a building to save energy also means designing a
building that is sensitive to nature. The result is a building that is better
for people.

Just as we feel more alive in a room open to sunlight and fresh air than
in one closed to the elements, E. O. Wilson speculates that we have an in-
nate need for contact with a wide variety of species. This need, which he
terms *biophilia,* reminds us that we are designed to live and adapt within

nature. The biophilia hypothesis "powerfully asserts that much of the human search for a coherent and fulfilling existence is intimately dependent upon our relationship to nature."[3] Ecological design responds to this need by bringing an elemental awareness of natural processes and interactions into even the urban context. It makes natural processes visible and active at levels of scale from the household to the neighborhood to the entire city.

Television nature shows, virtual reality, and books cannot substitute for real-time learning from a natural environment. One study of creative designers showed that many of them had spent lots of time during their childhoods playing in vacant lots in their neighborhoods. Here, away from the all-too-carefully designed order, they could experience, in the leftover space, weeds, bugs, and the cycle of unmanicured seasons. Here they had space to watch and dream.

Our de-natured cities stifle impulses toward biophilia. We may even be seeing the emergence of a new urban disease, what a psychiatrist friend calls *econoia,* or fear of living things. One time, an urban woman came as a student to the Farallones Rural Center, where residents used composting privies, grew their own food, and lived in solar cabins. Each day she seemed to be gone for a while and often wasn't at meals. After some weeks, she was asked about her absences, and she explained that every day she drove to town to use a flush toilet at the gas station and buy packaged food. The way we lived was "unnatural" to her.

Too often, the natural world is conceived as Nature with a capital "N," "out there" in remote mountain ranges, in rainforests, in the depths of the ocean. This has allowed us to conveniently believe that our activities can be carried out without consideration of their wider consequences. Weaving nature back into everyday life breaks down destructive dichotomies between the built world and wild nature. It reminds us of the ecological processes and biological diversity present even in the city. This kind of immediate, close-at-hand nature—a kind of small "n" nature—is one that needs to pervade culture.[4]

When we come to participate in organic processes as a necessary and intimate part of our lives, the awareness and motivation to protect the larger realms of big "N" Nature will be widespread and enormously powerful. On the other hand, if we fail to weave little "n" nature back into the everyday environment, big "N" Nature will become an expendable abstraction confined to television documentaries. Ecological design connects us to wider natural cycles, transforming our awareness of our place within nature.

In the same way that natural processes have been designed out of public view, the technology that supports urban life has been hidden. Typically, sewage plants, garbage dumps, aboveground gas storage tanks, slaughterhouses, and electrical generating and transmission stations are located in the poorest parts of town. Even benign technologies such as wind generators are considered a visual nuisance. We want clean energy, but perhaps not in our backyards. We have lived for some time now secure in the assumption that we are entitled to all the benefits of technology as long as someone less powerful puts up with the costs. This creates a strange schizophrenia in which our ideal is to consume sanitized versions of both nature and technology. That is indeed what the richer folk and nations get: a false and incomplete experience of both nature and technology, while others suffer the consequences.

Making nature visible is a way of reacquainting us with wider communities of life, but it also informs us about the ecological consequences of our activities. With a conventional storm-drain system, for instance, water quickly disappears into subterranean arteries, picking up various toxins along the way. The water is hidden, and so are the impacts of the system itself—contamination of downstream rivers or wetlands, altered hydrology, and decreased groundwater recharge. We can make the drainage system both visible and ecologically functional by letting water flow on the surface into drainage ponds like West Davis Ponds. We can preserve wetlands and stream corridors that act as natural sponges to absorb stormwaters. The delightful thing about such a design is that people love to watch it in action, rushing out in the rain to watch the water flow.

All of this suggests a new kind of aesthetic for the built environment, one that explicitly teaches people about the potentially symbiotic relationship between culture, nature, and design. It is a powerful approach, since new ideas are learned most rapidly when they can be expressed visually and experienced directly. The landscape architect Robert L. Thayer, Jr., has called this aesthetic *visual ecology*. This approach favors designed environments that can

- help us see and become more aware of the abstractions we superimpose on the land
- make complex natural processes visible and understandable
- unmask systems and processes that remain hidden from view
- emphasize our unrecognized connections to nature[5]

Many artists have found inventive ways to dramatize natural processes. Andy Goldsworthy works with simple materials—water, stones, leaves, sticks—to visualize wind, water flow, decay, and other phenomena. He speaks of his own work in this way: "Movement, change, light, growth and decay are the lifeblood of nature, the energies that I try to tap through my work. I need the shock of touch, the resistance of place, materials and weather, the earth as my source. I want to get under the surface. When I work with a leaf, rock, stick, it is not just that material in itself, it is an opening into the processes of life within and around it. When I leave it these processes continue."[6] His work is an active engagement with living processes.

In a parallel way, ecological design is linked to a visual ecology that celebrates our systems of water and energy, agriculture and production. This kind of visual ecology is emphasized in one of the Ecological Design Institute's current projects, The Real Goods Trading Company's Solar Living Center in Hopland, California (figures 19–24). The site consists of

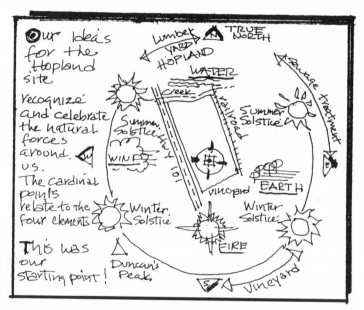

FIGURE 19. *Site analysis diagram for Real Goods Solar Living Center*

FIGURE 20. *Showroom and solar oasis*

FIGURE 21. *Showroom with highway at left, showing berm and landscaping*

FIGURE 22. *Pond and garden area on floodplain*

twelve acres on an agricultural floodplain. The program will include a showroom for ecological technologies, supporting facilities, and a demonstration landscape and garden that together inform people about the company's products and its ecological vision.

Both the site and the program offer strong possibilities for making natural processes visible. The silted, damaged stream that forms one end of the site is being restored to reflect its original riparian qualities. Constructed wetlands, ponds, and gardens fill the floodplain. The landscape design mimics the original variety of plant communities found in the

1. Native wetlands restoration
2. Demonstration garden
3. Ponds
4. Riparian restoration
5. Wooded berm
6. P.V. collectors
7. Solar oasis
8. Showroom

FIGURE 23. *Landscape plan for Real Goods Solar Living Center*

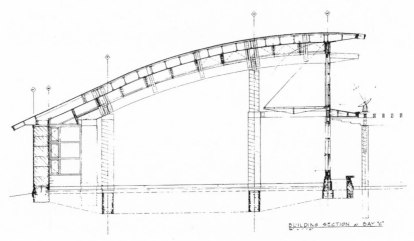

FIGURE 24. *"Bowstring" section of Real Goods headquarters*

area. Since the planting plan is spatially related to the seasons, it provides orienting clues to the sun's daily and seasonal paths. Water recycled from the copious on-site aquifer is a major element in the design. It provides summer cooling for outdoor spaces, soothing background sounds, and an animated path for visitors to follow. The site plan is a complex inter-weaving of ecotones that should prove to be favorable habitat for plants, animals, and people alike.

A building material was adopted only after strenuous consideration: Does it support wholeness? Is it a renewable resource? What is the energy embodied in its manufacture? Are the labor practices involved in its man-ufacture acceptable? Is it affordable? At first, cotton insulation seemed ideal, but pound for pound, cotton uses more pesticides, damages more soil and streams, and causes more health problems for workers than any other crop. Materials that passed review included rice-straw bales used for some walls, glue-laminated rafters made from locally reclaimed lumber and nontoxic glues, and a host of other recycled materials.

As part of the design process, a scale model of the facility was made and tested on a heliodon at Pacific Gas and Electric's Pacific Energy Center in San Francisco. The heliodon simulates the sun's path for any time or location, allowing designers to study natural lighting and solar gain. The design team made a videotape recording time-lapse sequences of the sun's path as it will appear to people inside the building. When the video was shown to Real Goods president John Shaeffer, he exclaimed, "Our employees will be lining up at 5:30 in the morning to get to work just to experience sunrise in there!" The south-facing building steps down in segments as it moves from west to east, allowing the morning sun to stream into high clerestory windows. The curved roof form is designed to evenly distribute daylight. The complex arrangements of building and landscape are designed to constantly remind people of the sun's path through the play of light and shadow and a host of orienting elements.

In the Real Goods project, all elements—architectural forms, building materials, ecological restoration efforts, water, landscaping, pathways, and public areas—provide subtle, ongoing lessons in sustainability. Even the entrance tiles are made of recycled solar cells. Like other effective ecological designs, it sets in motion processes that will continue to teach us year after year.

Ecological design transforms awareness by making nature visible. Spending time with ecologically designed buildings or environments, "one [increasingly] becomes aware of processes, patterns, and relationships."[7] At its best, ecological design provides concrete evidence of the pattern that connects us to the rhythms of life and place. It awakens our sense of belonging to a wider natural world. Ultimately, it brings us home.

Every great epoch in human history has been linked to the simultaneous development of landmark designs that manifest, nurture, and reinforce people's experience of their culture. Early agricultural empires built ceremonial sacred places whose spatial arrangements mirrored the elaborate hierarchies of their cosmology and social organization. In the Middle Ages in Europe, cathedrals—with their richness and complex coherence—embodied the essence and spirit of an all-encompassing Christianity. It is impossible to imagine the Renaissance mind without the boldness of Florence, the great city's public squares lined with monuments to a new scientific and entrepreneurial sensibility. The dawning Industrial Age created its own aesthetic, from Joseph Paxton's Crystal Palace to the great steam trains.

It is central to the concept of design to embody and mirror the dreams that create it. If our cities relegate nature to parks and designated open spaces, it is because our minds shut out nature from the rest of life. If our most visible monuments are highways, shopping malls, sprawling suburbs, office towers, and entertainment complexes, it is because our lives are dominated by movement, consumption, the search for individual realization, corporate power, and mass media. Our current environments speak louder than words. They suggest that our destinies will be determined by designs, technologies, and organizations over which we have no control. The continued destruction of nature—our kindred forms of life—is a holocaust that may well dwarf all other human experience. It is daily evidence of the folly we have designed for ourselves.

Ecological design reflects new dreams that can be embodied in new kinds of environments. These dreams are not of Armageddon nor Arcadia, but of a world where nature and culture, the living world and the designed world, are truly joined, each celebrated in the image of the other. We can create an Ecological Revolution every bit as profound as the preceding Industrial Revolution. The pieces are well understood, from energy efficiency and sustainable agriculture to ecological wastewater treatment and bioregional design.

We possess the collective potential to create environments that nurture both the human spirit and the more-than-human living world. The work awaits us.

### NOTES

1. Leonard Charles et al., "Bioregional Quiz," *Coevolutionary Quarterly*, no. 32 (winter 1981): 1.
2. Robin Grossinger, "The Land Beneath the City," *Annals of Earth* 12, no. 2 (1994): 24.

3. Stephen R. Kellert, "The Biological Basis for Human Values of Nature," in *The Biophilia Hypothesis,* ed. Stephen R. Kellert and Edward O. Wilson (Washington, D.C.: Island Press, 1993), 43.

4. The little "n," big "N" nature distinction originated with Susan Oyama. We are using it in a somewhat different sense. See Susan Oyama, "The Conceptualization of Nature: Nature as Design," in *Gaia 2: Emergence: The New Science of Becoming,* ed. William Irwin Thompson (Hudson, N.Y.: Lindisfarne Press, 1991), 171–84.

5. For the term *visual ecology,* see Robert L. Thayer, Jr., "Visual Ecology: Revitalizing the Aesthetics of Landscape Architecture," *Landscape* 20, no. 2 (1976): 37–43. A valuable treatment of visual ecology is provided by David Robinson in *Making Nature Visible: The Art of Visual Ecology,* a Masters of Landscape Architecture professional report, Univ. of California at Berkeley, 1993.

6. Andy Goldsworthy, introduction to *Andy Goldsworthy: A Collaboration with Nature* (New York: Harry N. Abrams, 1990).

7. John Todd and Nancy Jack Todd, *Tomorrow Is Our Permanent Address: The Search for an Ecological Science of Design as Embodied in the Bioshelter* (New York: Harper & Row, 1980), 151.

# RESOURCE GUIDE FOR ECOLOGICAL DESIGN

Some of the most active and innovative organizations and projects in the field of ecological design are listed on the following pages. Books are listed separately in the Bibliography.

We would appreciate any update information and suggestions for additions to this list. In a bioregional spirit, it focuses on our home state of California and on the United States, but we would like to create a more geographically inclusive list. You can write to us in care of the Ecological Design Institute, Suite 185, Ten Libertyship Way, Sausalito, CA 94965.

A new organization, the International Ecological Design Society, serves as a clearinghouse and "trade association" for ecological design. For information, contact the society at P.O. Box 11645, Berkeley, CA 94712; telephone: (510) 869-5015, E-mail: ecodesign@igc.apc.org. The society will begin publishing the quarterly *Journal of Ecological Design* in spring 1996. It is also pursuing innovative educational opportunities in ecological design.

*Sim Van der Ryn and Stuart Cowan*

Arcata Marsh and Wildlife Sanctuary
Arcata, CA
*A marsh that serves as the final step in purifying Arcata's wastewater, as well as a rich bird habitat and delightful recreation spot.*

Architects/Designers/Planners for Social Responsibility (ADPSR)
65 Bleecker Street
New York, NY 10012
(212) 924-7893
*This wide-ranging group of designers focuses on sustainability as a core concern.*

Arcosanti
HC 74, P.O. Box 4136
Mayer, AZ 86333
(520) 632-7135
*Paolo Soleri, Architect. A compact intentional community in the Arizona desert consisting of high-density dwellings and dedicated to frugal resource use.*

Audubon Building, The
700 Broadway
New York, NY
*Croxton Collaborative, Architects. This ecological retrofit of a turn-of-the century office building is well documented in* Audubon House, *by the National Audubon Society and the Croxton Collaborative (see Bibliography).*

Boyne River Natural Science School
Shelbourne, Ontario, Canada
(519) 925-3913
*Douglas B. Pollard, Architect. An ecology center for the schoolchildren of Toronto, it features excellent passive solar design and a living machine for treating wastewater.*

Cathedral of Saint John the Divine
1047 Amsterdam Avenue at 112th Street
New York, NY 10025
(212) 316-7400
*Under the leadership of Dean James Morton, the church has undertaken many projects connecting spirituality and the environment.*

Center for Agroecology and Sustainable Food Systems
Farm and Garden
University of California, Santa Cruz
1156 High Street
Santa Cruz, CA 95076
(408) 459-4140
*Excellent research program on the ecological context of sustainable agriculture.*

Center for Maximum Potential Building Systems (Max's Pot)
8604 F.M. 969
Austin, TX 78724
(512) 928-4786
*Investigates alternative building materials, the use of local resources, and advanced energy and wastewater systems for buildings.*

Center for Regenerative Studies
California State Polytechnic University
3801 West Temple Avenue
Pomona, CA 91768
(909) 468-1705
*Now in the first stage of construction, this will eventually be a living and working environment for ninety students, who will try to live self-sufficiently on the campus, growing their own food, monitoring energy use, and so forth.*

Center for Resourceful Building Technology
P.O. Box 3866
Missoula, MT 59806
(406) 549-7678
*This group does important research on the environmental impacts of building materials and publishes the* Guide to Resource Efficient Building Elements (GREBE) *catalog.*

CRATerre-EAG (Centre International de la Construction en Terre École d'Architecture Grenoble)
10 Galerie des Baladins
BP 2636, F-38036
Grenoble Cedex 2, France
33-76-40-66-25
*Investigates the use of earth as a building material and works to maintain indigenous building methods worldwide.*

Cerro Gordo
c/o Cerro Gordo Town Forum
Dorena Lake, P.O. Box 569
Cottage Grove, OR 97424
(503) 942-7720
*An intentional community that is keeping 90 percent of its land in open space and is building houses from wood sustainably harvested on-site.*

Cob Cottage Company
P.O. Box 123
Cottage Grove, OR 97424
*This small group is reviving the art of building with cob, a straw-clay mixture.*

CoHousing Company, The
1250 Addison Street #13
Berkeley, CA 94702
(510) 549-9980
*Provides technical assistance to groups interested in cooperative housing, in which several individual dwellings share common living and eating spaces.*

Congress of New Urbanism (CNU)
c/o Peter Calthorpe
246 First Street, Suite 400
San Francisco, CA 94105
*A group of planners, architects, landscape architects, engineers, developers, and others who are trying to formulate principles for ecological city building and rebuilding, set standards, and share information.*

Crowley Sewage Treatment Plant
Crowley, LA
*Bill Wolverton, Consulting Biologist; Maders-Miers Engineering, Engineers. Waste-water for this town of eighteen thousand is treated by a wetlands system. Water flows through large ponds, two marshes, and a rock-reed filter before it is safely released in a nearby bayou.*

Curitiba
Curitiba, Brazil
*Mayor Jaimie Lerner has helped turn Curitiba into a world leader in recycling, public transit, ecological restoration, and green industry.*

Design Center for American Urban Landscape
University of Minnesota
College of Architecture and Landscape Architecture
1313 Fifth Street SE, Suite 222
Minneapolis, MN 55414
(612) 627-1850
*William Morrish and colleagues work with local citizens on ecological planning projects.*

Ecological Design Institute, The
10 Libertyship Way, Suite 185
Sausalito, CA 94965
(415) 332-5806
*Provides a comprehensive range of ecological design services, performs research, and creates educational programs.*

Ecolonia
Informatiecentrum
Postbus 666
2400 AR Alphen aan den Rijn, The Netherlands
31-046-595-295
*A government-sponsored experiment in environmentally sensitive solar housing. The small village features innovative use of materials and high levels of energy efficiency.*

Environmental Protection Encouragement Agency (EPEA)
Feldstrasse 36
D-2000 Hamburg 38, Germany
*Under the leadership of "green chemist" Michael Braungart, the EPEA does pioneering research on the creation of environmentally safe chemical pathways for products.*

*Flow City*
Marine Transfer Station
West Fifty-ninth Street at the Hudson River
New York, NY
*Mierle Ukeles, Artist. This ambitious installation documents the flows of waste in the city of New York.*

Gaia Institute
Cathedral of Saint John the Divine
1047 Amsterdam Avenue at 112th Street
New York, NY 10025
*A small, innovative group of designers and biologists who undertake visionary ecological restoration projects and develop new ecological technologies.*

Green Builder Program
City of Austin
Environment and Conservation Service Department
206 East Ninth Street, Suite 17.102
Austin, TX 78701
*A series of checklists and worksheets provided by the city of Austin allows builders to assess the sustainability of their projects.*

Haymount
Haymount, VA
*Duany-Plater-Zyberk (DPZ), Planners. An innovative new town featuring neo-tradi-tional town-planning guidelines, a constructed wetland, and numerous wildlife areas.*

ING Bank
Communications Department
Internal Communications and Publications Section
P.O. Box 1800
1000 BV Amsterdam, The Netherlands
31-020-563-9111
*Alberts and Van Huut, Architects. Large-scale bank that uses 90 percent less energy than a conventional building; has advanced daylighting features, remarkable gardens, and*

*water sculptures; and is considered one of the most user friendly office buildings in the world.*

Institute for Local Self-Reliance
2425 Eighteenth Street NW
Washington, DC 20009
(202) 232-4108
*Provides assistance to communities interested in becoming more self-sufficient. Has pioneered several exceptional recycling programs.*

Intermediate Technology Development Group (ITDG)
103-105 Southampton Row
London WC1 B4H4, United Kingdom
*Promotes appropriate technology in the spirit of E. F. Schumacher.*

International Ecological Design Society (IEDS)
P.O. Box 11645
Berkeley, CA 94712
(510) 869-5015
*A clearinghouse and trade association for ecological design.*

International Society for Ecological Economics
P.O. Box 1589
Solomons, MD 20688
*A clearinghouse for ecologists and economists seeking common ground. Publishes the* Journal of Ecological Economics.

Kalundborg Industrial Ecosystem
Kalundborg, Denmark
*A group of industrial facilities that have found ways to effectively link their flows of energy and materials.*

Ladakh Project, The
c/o International Society for Ecology and Culture
P.O. Box 9745
Berkeley, CA 94709
(510) 527-3873
*Helena Norberg-Hodge is working to preserve traditional patterns of agriculture, building, and settlement in Ladakh, India. The group is also selectively introducing some forms of appropriate technology.*

Land Institute, The
2440 East Waterwell Road
Salina, KS 67401
(913) 823-5376
*Wes Jackson and colleagues perform innovative research intended to create a sustainable prairie agriculture based on native perennial species.*

Laredo Demonstration Blueprint Farm
Laredo, TX
(512) 928-4786
*Center for Maximum Potential Building Systems, Principal Designer. The Blueprint Farm demonstrates several ecological technologies, including on-site wastewater treatment and cisterns. It also makes extensive use of recycled and local materials.*

Matfield Green
c/o The Land Institute
2440 East Waterwell Road
Salina, KS 67401
(913) 823-5376
*An attempt to create a sustainable local economy in the small Kansas town of Matfield Green. The experiment is also a pioneering attempt to perform ecological accounting at the community scale.*

Natural Building Network
P.O. Box 1110
Sebastopol, CA 95473
*An association of builders, designers, and architects working with natural building materials and energy-efficient design.*

Natural Step Foundation, The
Amiralitetshuset, Skeppsholmen
111 49 Stockholm, Sweden
*An innovative project that helped hundreds of Sweden's leading scientists reach a consensus on environmental issues. The results have been summarized in a beautiful, illustrated document distributed to every household in Sweden.*

O2
Best reached on the Internet at 74241.667@compuserve.com.
*A European network of innovative product designers and ecological designers.*

Oasis Biocompatible Products
5 San Marcos Trout Club
Santa Barbara, CA 93105
(805) 967-3222
*Provides technical information on reclaiming graywater (water from showers and sinks).*

Ocean Arks International (OAI)
1 Locust Street
Falmouth, MA 02540
(508) 540-6801
*John Todd and associates have built innovative ecological wastewater treatment systems in Providence, Rhode Island; Frederick, Maryland; and other locations.*

Pacific Energy Center
Pacific Gas and Electric Company
851 Howard Street
San Francisco, CA 94103
(415) 973-7268
*This demonstration center for energy-efficient technologies also provides assistance to architects interested in testing the energy performance of their designs.*

## PERMACULTURE

Drylands Permaculture Institute
P.O. Box 133
Pearce, AZ 85625

Permaculture Institute, The
P.O. Box 1
Tyalgum NSW 2484, Australia

Permaculture Institute of Northern California, The
P.O. Box 341
Point Reyes Station, CA 94956
(415) 663-9090

*An international movement in sustainable agriculture and whole systems design. Offers intensive two-week courses that immerse students in a framework closely related to that of ecological design. The institutes listed are just three of the dozens of permaculture organizations located worldwide.*

Real Goods Trading Company Solar Living Center
Hopland, CA
*Ecological Design Institute, Architects. A showcase for the Real Goods product line of eco-logical technologies. The headquarters will be off the grid, generating its own energy, and features innovative landscaping.*

Resource Renewal Institute
Fort Mason Center
Building A
San Francisco, CA 94123
(415) 928-3774
*A group working toward creating a "green plan," or strategic environmental plan, for the United States. Publicizes existing green plans in Canada, Denmark, the Nether-lands, and other countries.*

Rocky Mountain Institute (RMI)
1739 Snowmass Creek Road
Snowmass, CO 81654
(303) 927-3128
*Steven Conger and the Aspen Design Group, Architects. This institute does excellent re-search on energy efficiency and energy policy. Their headquarters is a masterpiece of pas-sive solar design.*

Schumacher College
The Old Postern
Dartington, Totnes
Devon TQ9 6EA, United Kingdom
*Offers short courses by internationally renowned teachers on topics of relevance to ecolog-ical design.*

SITE (Sculpture In The Environment)
632 Broadway
New York, NY 10012
(212) 254-8300
*A group of architects and artists designing buildings and landscapes that fuse structure and nature.*

Seeds of Change
P.O. Box 15700
Santa Fe, NM 87506
(505) 983-8956
*An organic seed company that specializes in preserving genetic variability and biodiversity. Seeds of Change sponsors an excellent annual conference on "bioneers," people working to regenerate ecosystems and create restorative forms of business.*

606 Studio
California State Polytechnic University
3801 West Temple Avenue
Pomona, CA 91768
*Under the guidance of John Tillman Lyle, graduate students in landscape architecture tackle complex planning and design problems in this studio.*

Society for Ecological Restoration
University of Wisconsin–Madison Arboretum
1207 Seminole Highway
Madison, WI 53711
*An international society for those involved in ecological restoration and ecosystem management. Publishes the essential* Restoration & Management Notes.

Stensund Wastewater Aquaculture
Stensund Folk College
S-619 00 Trosa, Sweden
46-0156-16490
*Bengt Warne, Architect. Features an excellent ecological wastewater treatment facility that is partly run by the students.*

Sustainable Seattle
Young Men's Christian Association, Metro Center
909 Fourth Avenue
Seattle, WA 98104
(206) 382-5013
*A grassroots group that monitors the health of the Seattle area while promoting and envisioning sustainable alternatives.*

University of Virginia School of Architecture
Campbell Hall
Charlottesville, VA 22903
(804) 924-3715
*Under the direction of William McDonough, the school is instituting an innovative interdisciplinary program in sustainable design.*

Urban Ecology
405 Fourteenth Street, Suite 701
Oakland, CA 94612
(510) 251-6330
*Currently working on a major sustainability study of the San Francisco Bay Area. The group publishes a newsletter on ecological cities,* The Urban Ecologist.

Urban Habitat
c/o Earth Island Institute
300 Broadway, Suite 28
San Francisco, CA 94133
(415) 788-3666
*A project that addresses issues of environmental justice. It publishes the journal* Race, Poverty, and the Environment.

Village Homes
Davis, CA
*Michael and Judy Corbett, Developers. A beautifully landscaped cluster of solar homes. Features copious fruit trees, surface drainage, and wonderful commons spaces.*

West Davis Ponds
Davis, CA
*An artfully contoured drainage retention basin. Its miniature islands provide habitat for dozens of bird species.*

Whidbey Institute
P.O. Box 529
Clinton, WA 98236
(360) 341-5430
*This educational organization bridges environmental and spiritual concerns.*

Wildcat Creek
c/o California Natural Resources Foundation
1250 Addison Street #107
Berkeley, CA 94702
(510) 848-2211
*Ann Riley has been working on a grassroots effort to restore Wildcat and San Pablo Creeks in North Richmond, California. The design will provide high levels of flood control and numerous recreational amenities.*

Wildlands Project, The
P.O. Box 1276
McMinnville, OR 97128
(503) 434-9848
*The project is working on a long-term biodiversity recovery plan for North America. It has developed sophisticated land-use maps to document its vision.*

Yuba Watershed Institute
17790 Tyler Foote Road
Nevada City, CA 95959
(916) 478-0817
*A grassroots forest stewardship project that has made excellent use of geographical information systems (GIS) to jointly manage Bureau of Land Management lands.*

# BIBLIOGRAPHY

Aberley, Doug, ed. *Boundaries of Home: Mapping for Local Empowerment.* Gabriola Island, British Columbia: New Society Publishers, 1993. This informative guide explains the use of community-based mapping techniques for understanding bioregions.

_____, ed. *Futures by Design: The Practice of Ecological Planning.* Gabriola Island, British Columbia: New Society Publishers, 1994. An accessible anthology on ecological planning methods.

Adey, Walter. *Dynamic Aquaria: Building Living Ecosystems.* San Diego: Academic Press, 1991. A wonderful handbook for building aquatic microcosms.

Alexander, Christopher, et al. *A Pattern Language.* New York: Oxford Univ. Press, 1977. This design classic examines the patterns that make for good building at levels of scale ranging from furniture details to cities.

_____. *The Timeless Way of Building.* New York: Oxford Univ. Press, 1979. The themes of *A Pattern Language* are further developed.

_____. *The Nature of Order.* New York: Oxford Univ. Press, forthcoming. An extended meditation on the patterns of wholeness within nature and design.

Allen, T. F. H., and Thomas W. Hoekstra. *Toward a Unified Ecology.* New York: Columbia Univ. Press, 1992. An overview of ecology from a scale-linking perspective.

Altieri, Miguel. *Agroecology: The Scientific Basis of Alternative Agriculture.* Boulder, Colo.: Westview Press, 1987. An integration of traditional farming with contemporary ecological science.

Badiner, Allan Hunt, ed. *Dharma Gaia: A Harvest of Essays in Buddhism and Ecology.* Berkeley: Parallax Press, 1990. Collection of essays linking Buddhist awareness to ecological awareness.

Bateson, Gregory. *Steps to an Ecology of Mind*. New York: Ballantine Books, 1972. An investigation of evolution and the marks it has left on the human mind: the patterns that connect our cognitive and cultural processes to natural processes.

Berry, Thomas. *The Dream of the Earth*. San Francisco: Sierra Club Books, 1990. A beautiful meditation on the role of humans in planetary evolution.

Berry, Wendell. *The Unsettling of America: Culture and Agriculture*. San Francisco: Sierra Club Books, 1977. A farmer, poet, and tireless advocate for appropriate scale examines the transition from family farms to agribusiness.

_____. *The Gift of Good Land: Further Essays Cultural and Agricultural*. San Francisco: North Point Press, 1981. Extraordinary essays on farming and sustainability. Berry's books cannot be recommended highly enough.

Botkin, Daniel B. *Discordant Harmonies: A New Ecology for the Twenty-first Century*. New York: Oxford Univ. Press, 1990. An exploration of complexity and ecology.

Briggs, John. *Fractals: The Patterns of Chaos: Discovering a New Aesthetic of Art, Science, and Nature*. New York: Simon & Schuster, 1992. A lavishly illustrated presentation of the work of artists and scientists taking their inspiration from fractals and chaos theory.

Cajete, Gregory. *Look to the Mountain: An Ecology of Indigenous Education*. Durango, Colo.: Kivaki Press, 1994. An inspired examination of place-based approaches to education.

Calatrava, Santiago. *Dynamic Equilibrium: Recent Projects*. Zurich: Architectural Publishers, 1992. Remarkable designs from an architect-engineer deeply inspired by natural form.

Calthorpe, Peter. *The Next American Metropolis: Ecology, Community, and the American Dream*. New York: Princeton Architectural Press, 1993. A perceptive study of ecologically sensitive approaches to town planning. Clearly and simply presented.

Canfield, Christopher, ed. *Report of the First International Ecological City Conference*. Berkeley: Urban Ecology; Dorena Lake, Ore.: Cerro Gordo Town Forum, 1990. Short summaries of talks given at the conference. Good introduction to ecocities.

Chahroudi, Day. "Buildings as Organisms." In *Soft-Tech,* edited by J. Baldwin and Stewart Brand, 40–5. London: Penguin Books, 1978. Discussion of climate control utilizing three new materials based on natural analogues.

Coates, Gary J., ed. *Resettling America: Energy, Ecology, and Community*. Andover, Mass.: Brick House, 1981. A comprehensive anthology on local self-reliance.

Costanza, Robert, ed. *Ecological Economics: The Science and Management of Sustainability*. New York: Columbia Univ. Press, 1991. One of the better books on the new ecological economics. Presents theory and useful case studies.

Daly, Herman E., and John B. Cobb, Jr. *For the Common Good: Redirecting the Economy Toward Community, the Environment, and a Sustainable Future*. Boston: Beacon Press, 1989. Fundamental ideas on building a sustainable economy responsive to issues of ecology and equity.

Diamond, Irene, and Gloria Feman Orenstein, eds. *Reweaving the World: The Emergence of Ecofeminism*. San Francisco: Sierra Club Books, 1990. An excellent anthology on ecofeminism, which connects ecological and feminist concerns.

Duany, Andres, and Elizabeth Plater-Zyberk. *Towns and Town-Making Principles*. New York: Rizzoli, 1991. An interesting attempt to adapt traditional town-planning principles to the contemporary context.

Eagan, David J., and David W. Orr, eds. "The Campus and Environmental Responsibility," special issue of *New Directions for Higher Education*, no. 77 (spring 1992). A series of case studies on student-led, campuswide environmental audits.

Ecological Design Project, The. *Ecological Design: Inventing the Future*. New York: The Ecological Design Project, 1994. Videocassette. This hour-long video provides a clear overview of ecological design.

Etnier, Carl, and Björn Gutterstam, eds. *Ecological Engineering for Wastewater Treatment*. Gothenburg, Sweden: Bokskogen, 1991. Proceedings from a fruitful Swedish conference on ecological wastewater treatment. Covers a wide range of systems, from living machines to constructed wetlands.

Fathy, Hassan. *Architecture for the Poor: An Experiment in Rural Egypt*. Chicago: Univ. of Chicago Press, 1973. The story of an attempt to build a community with local labor and materials.

Fiedler, Peggy L., and Subodh K. Jain, eds. *Conservation Biology: The Theory and Practice of Nature Conservation, Preservation, and Management*. New York: Chapman & Hall, 1992. A good anthology on methods for preserving biological diversity.

Fisk, Pliny. "Bioregions and Biotechnologies: A New Planning Tool for Stable State Economic Development." Austin: Center for Maximum Potential Building Systems, 1983. This highly recommended report offers a visionary approach to bioregional-level planning.

Forman, R. T. T. *Landscape Ecology*. New York: John Wiley & Sons, 1986. A solid introduction to the field of landscape ecology, which treats human disturbances in the context of ecological processes.

Frosch, Robert A., and Nicholas E. Gallopoulos. "Strategies for Manufacturing." *Scientific American* 261, no. 3 (September 1989). A good early overview of industrial ecology.

Fukuoka, Masanobu. *The One-Straw Revolution.* Emmaus, Pa.: Rodale Press, 1978. Classic approach to organic agriculture.

Gablik, Suzi. *The Reenchantment of Art.* New York: Thames and Hudson, 1991. A discussion of artists who infuse their work with community, ecological, and spiritual dimensions.

Goldsworthy, Andy. *Andy Goldsworthy: A Collaboration with Nature.* New York: Harry N. Abrams, 1990. A visionary artist who works with ice, leaves, rocks, and whatever else is at hand to create ephemeral, biodegradable art.

Gordon, David, ed. *Green Cities: Ecologically Sound Approaches to Urban Spaces.* Montreal: Black Rose, 1990. Compendium of ideas on ecological cities.

Grumbine, R. Edward. *Ghost Bears: Exploring the Biodiversity Crisis.* Washington, D.C.: Island Press, 1992. Biodiversity and land-use issues are highlighted by the example of the endangered grizzly bear.

Hammer, Donald A., ed. *Constructed Wetlands for Wastewater Treatment: Municipal, Industrial, and Agricultural.* Chelsea, Mich.: Lewis, 1989. A valuable encyclopedia of constructed wetlands.

Harrison, Helen Mayer, and Newton Harrison. *The Lagoon Cycle.* Ithaca: Cornell Univ., 1985. Documents an extraordinary, ongoing ecological art project that encompasses everything from ancient water systems in Sri Lanka to new kinds of aquaculture to meditations on reclaiming damaged agricultural lands.

Harte, John, et al. *Toxics A to Z: A Guide to Everyday Pollution Hazards.* Berkeley and Los Angeles: Univ. of California Press, 1991. An clear introduction to toxic substances, including a long reference section on the most common forms.

Hawken, Paul. *The Ecology of Commerce: A Declaration of Sustainability.* New York: HarperCollins, 1993. A regenerative vision of business that outlines a way to properly account for ecological costs within our existing system of commerce.

Hough, Michael. *City Form and Natural Processes: Towards an Urban Vernacular.* New York: Van Nostrand Reinhold, 1984. Examines the prospects for incorporating natural processes in an urban setting.

Hull, Fritz, ed. *Earth & Spirit: The Environmental Dimension of the Spiritual Crisis.* New York: Continuum, 1993. A rich collection of essays connecting ecology and spirituality.

Illich, Ivan. *Tools for Conviviality.* New York: Harper & Row, 1973. A study of the diminishing returns of technological systems beyond a certain scale.

Jackson, Wes. *New Roots for Agriculture.* San Francisco: Friends of the Earth, 1980. An appraisal of the prospects for sustainable agriculture.

_____. *Becoming Native to This Place.* Lexington: Univ. Press of Kentucky, 1994. Thoughts on what it would require for Americans to truly become native to their adopted place.

Jackson, Wes, Wendell Berry, and Bruce Colman, eds. *Meeting the Expectations of the Land: Essays in Sustainable Agriculture and Stewardship.* San Francisco: North Point Press, 1984. A valuable collection of essays on sustainable agriculture.

Jacobs, Jane. *The Economy of Cities.* New York: Random House, 1969. Presents clear arguments for cities that are more self-reliant.

Jantsch, Eric. *The Self-Organizing Universe: Scientific and Human Implications of the Emerging Paradigm of Evolution.* Oxford: Pergamon Press, 1980. An idiosyncratic discussion of self-organization and its social implications.

Johansson, Allan. *Clean Technology.* Boca Raton, Fla.: Lewis, 1992. Clear account of pollution reduction and elimination techniques.

Johansson, Thomas B., et al. *Renewable Energy: Sources for Fuels and Electricity.* Washington, D.C.: Island Press, 1993. An authoritative reference on renewable energy.

Katz, Michael, William P. Marsh, and Gail Gordon Thompson, eds. *Earth's Answer: Explorations of Planetary Culture at the Lindisfarne Conferences.* New York: Harper & Row, 1977. A seminal collection of thoughts about planetary survival.

Kauffman, Stuart A. *Origins of Order: Self-Organization and Selection in Evolution.* Oxford: Oxford Univ. Press, 1993. A demanding study of the deep roots of co-evolution and biodiversity. A keystone of the complex systems literature.

Kaza, Stephanie. *The Attentive Heart: Conversations with Trees.* New York: Ballantine Books, 1993. Beautiful meditations on trees, with accompanying woodcuts. Rich and rewarding.

Kemf, Elizabeth, ed. *The Law of the Mother: Protecting Indigenous Peoples in Protected Areas.* San Francisco: Sierra Club Books, 1993. A collection of case studies on the biosphere reserve concept, which attempts to meet the needs of indigenous people while protecting biodiversity.

Kemmis, Daniel. *Community and the Politics of Place.* Norman: Univ. of Oklahoma Press, 1990. A wise book on reviving local economies and town-hall politics written by the mayor of Missoula, Montana.

Ladakh Project, The. *Ecological Steps Towards a Sustainable Future.* Bristol, England: The Ladakh Project, 1991. A progress report on Helena Norberg-Hodge's alternative development project in Ladakh, a region in northern India.

Leopold, Aldo. *A Sand County Almanac.* New York: Oxford Univ. Press, 1948. Eloquent argument for a "land ethic" capable of preserving ecosystems.

Lewin, Roger. *Complexity: Life at the Edge of Chaos.* New York: Macmillan, 1992. An examination of the deep structure of biodiversity as revealed in historical extinction events.

Lovelock, James. *The Ages of Gaia: A Biography of Our Living Earth.* New York: Bantam Books, 1990. An overview of Gaia theory by one of its founders.

Lovins, Amory. *Soft Energy Paths.* New York: Harper & Row, 1977. Foundation of least-cost end-use analysis. Demonstrates conclusively that matching energy production to use results in enormous increases in efficiency.

Lyle, John Tillman. *Design for Human Ecosystems: Landscape, Land Use, and Natural Resources.* New York: Van Nostrand Reinhold, 1985. A thorough study of ecological design at the landscape scale.

_____. *Regenerative Design for Sustainable Development.* New York: John Wiley & Sons, 1994. A compendium of ecological design methods and strategies.

Macy, Joanna. *The World as Lover, the World as Self.* Berkeley: Parallax Press, 1991. A powerful union of Buddhism, deep ecology, and general systems theory.

Mandelbrot, B. B. *The Fractal Geometry of Nature.* New York: W. H. Freeman, 1982. An exploration of fractal geometry, full of clever examples and speculations.

Mander, Jerry. *In the Absence of the Sacred: The Failure of Technology and the Survival of the Indian Nations.* San Francisco: Sierra Club Books, 1991. A search for an ethics of technology.

Margolin, Malcolm. *The Earth Manual: How to Work on Wild Land Without Taming It.* Berkeley: Heyday Books, 1985. A clear and beautiful discussion on land stewardship.

Margulis, Lynn, and Dorion Sagan. *Microcosmos: Four Billion Years of Microbial Evolution.* New York: Simon & Schuster, 1986. A history of life on Earth, emphasizing the role of bacteria in evolution.

Matilsky, Barbara. *Fragile Ecologies: Contemporary Artists' Interpretations and Solutions.* New York: Rizzoli, 1992. Catalog for a traveling exhibit of profoundly inspiring ecological art by artists who are integrating ecological restoration, natural flows, and plants into their work. Truly a primer on making nature visible, it is highly recommended.

Mazria, Edward. *The Passive Solar Home Book.* Emmaus, Pa.: Rodale Press, 1979. A guide to the principles of solar architecture.

McHarg, Ian. *Design with Nature.* Garden City, N.Y.: Natural History Press, 1969. A seminal text on ecological design. Passionate, beautifully illustrated, and clear, it is mainly concerned with the landscape scale.

McKenzie, Dorothy. *Design for the Environment.* New York: Rizzoli, 1991. Presents a wide range of environmentally sensitive design examples, from textile design to product design to villages.

Meadows, Donella, et al. *Beyond the Limits: Confronting Global Collapse and Envisioning a Sustainable Future.* Post Mills, Vt.: Chelsea Green, 1992. A clear diagnosis of the global environmental crisis.

Mitsch, William J., and S. E. Jørgensen, eds. *Ecological Engineering: An Introduction to Ecotechnology.* New York: John Wiley & Sons, 1989. Textbook-level introduction to ecological wastewater treatment and other applications of ecological engineering.

Mollison, Bill. *Permaculture: A Practical Guide for a Sustainable Future.* Washington, D.C.: Island Press, 1990. A comprehensive introduction to designing for self-sufficiency based on the principles of permaculture, or "permanent agriculture."

Morris, David, and Irshad Ahmed. *The Carbohydrate Economy: Making Chemicals and Industrial Materials from Plant Matter.* Washington, D.C.: Institute for Local Self-Reliance, 1992. Examines the possibility of transforming industrial chemicals from a petroleum base to a nontoxic, carbohydrate base.

Mumford, Lewis. *The City in History: Its Origins and Transformations, and Its Prospects.* New York: Harcourt, Brace & World, 1961. The definitive historical and philosophical study of the city.

_____. *The Myth of the Machine.* 2 vols. New York: Harcourt, Brace & World, 1967–70. A masterful and comprehensive study of technology and culture.

Nabhan, Gary Paul. *The Desert Smells Like Rain: A Naturalist in Papago Indian Country.* San Francisco: North Point Press, 1982. An elegant study of traditional Papago agriculture.

_____. *Enduring Seeds: Native American Agriculture and Wild Plant Conservation.* San Francisco: North Point Press, 1989. A rich study of traditional agriculture and the role of seed propagation in preserving biodiversity.

Nabokov, Peter, and Robert Easton. *Native American Architecture.* New York: Oxford Univ. Press, 1989. A beautifully illustrated study of indigenous architecture in North America.

National Academy of Engineering. *Technology and Environment.* Washington, D.C.: National Academy Press, 1989. Good collection of technical articles on an industrial ecology theme.

National Audubon Society and Croxton Collaborative, Architects. *Audubon House: Building the Environmentally Responsible, Energy-Efficient Office.* New York: John Wiley & Sons, 1994. A detailed case study of an ecologically sound renovation in New York City.

National Park Service. *Guiding Principles of Sustainable Design*. Denver: National Park Service, 1993. A clear and practical introduction to sustainable design with special reference to the Park Service's ongoing initiatives.

Nicolis, Gregoire, and Ilya Prigogine. *Exploring Complexity: An Introduction*. New York: W. H. Freeman, 1989. An introduction to complex systems requiring relatively little mathematics.

Nilsen, Richard, ed. *Helping Nature Heal: An Introduction to Environmental Restoration*. Berkeley: Ten Speed Press, 1991. A nontechnical overview of the art of restoration.

Norberg-Hodge, Helena. *Ancient Futures: Learning from Ladakh*. San Francisco: Sierra Club Books, 1991. Profoundly moving study of the debilitating effects of forced modernization in Ladakh, a state in northern India.

Norgaard, Richard. *Development Betrayed: The End of Progress and a Coevolutionary Revisioning of the Future*. New York: Routledge, 1994. A dense study of sustainability's philosophical foundations.

Noss, Reed F., and Allen Y. Cooperrider. *Saving Nature's Legacy: Protecting and Restoring Biodiversity*. Washington, D.C.: Island Press, 1994. Sound strategies for maintaining biological diversity.

Odum, Howard T. *Environment, Power, and Society*. New York: John Wiley & Sons, 1971. A prescient book that has influenced a generation of ecological engineers with its call to work with the self-designing tendencies of ecosystems.

Olkowski, Helga, et al. *The Integral Urban House: Self-Reliant Living in the City*. San Francisco: Sierra Club Books, 1979. A nuts-and-bolts account of a partially self-sufficient house developed in Berkeley during the 1970s.

Orr, David W. *Ecological Literacy: Education and the Transition to a Postmodern World*. Albany: State Univ. of New York Press, 1992. A courageous and challenging vision of an ecological curriculum predicated on place. Indispensable; the pedagogical equivalent of ecological design. Features a wonderful reading list for developing ecological literacy.

Platt, Rutherford H., Rowan A. Rowntree, and Pamela C. Muick, eds. *The Ecological City: Preserving and Restoring Urban Biodiversity*. Amherst: Univ. of Massachusetts Press, 1994. A collection of papers on weaving nature into the urban landscape.

Prigogine, Ilya, and Isabelle Stengers. *Order Out of Chaos: Man's New Dialogue with Nature*. New York: Bantam Books, 1977. Explains limits of conventional thermodynamics; demonstrates that open systems can maintain complex structures far from equilibrium.

*Proceedings of the National Academy of Sciences* 89, no. 3 (1 February 1992). This special issue devoted to industrial ecology, a collection of papers from an important colloquium, provides an overview of the field.

Roszak, Theodore. *The Voice of the Earth.* New York: Simon & Schuster, 1992. Proposes a new kind of "ecopsychology."

Sachs, Wolfgang. *The Development Dictionary: A Guide to Knowledge as Power.* London: Zed Books, 1992. This series of essay-length definitions of key development terms brilliantly critiques conventional notions of "development."

_____. ed. *Global Ecology: A New Arena of Political Conflict.* London: Zed Books, 1993. A sobering study of the limitations of the current global environmental discourse.

Sale, Kirkpatrick. *Human Scale.* New York: Putnam, 1982. A study of the influence of scale on design and governance.

Schneider, Stephen H., and Penelope J. Boston, eds. *Scientists on Gaia.* Cambridge: MIT Press, 1991. An overview of the science behind Gaia theory.

Schumacher, E. F. *Small Is Beautiful.* New York: Harper & Row, 1973. A deeply sane book about the insanities of economics and a way out. Launched the appropriate-technology movement.

Schwenk, Theodor. *Sensitive Chaos: The Creation of Flowing Forms in Water and Air.* New York: Schoken Books, 1976. Beautifully illustrated study of the dynamics of water and air.

Shiva, Vandana. *Staying Alive: Woman, Ecology and Development.* London: Zed Books, 1988. A devastating discussion of science as power in the context of forest policy in India.

_____. *Monocultures of the Mind: Perspectives on Biodiversity and Biotechnology.* London: Zed Books, 1993. Examines the link between cultural and biological diversity.

Snyder, Gary. *The Practice of the Wild.* San Francisco: North Point Press, 1990. In a series of elegant essays demonstrating the poet's touch, Snyder maps the growth of culture outward from a deep sense of place.

Soule, Judith D., and Jon K. Piper. *Farming in Nature's Image: An Ecological Approach to Agriculture.* Washington, D.C.: Island Press, 1992. An exploration of the Land Institute's attempts to create truly sustainable agriculture by mimicking the structures and functions of healthy ecosystems.

Sprin, Anne Whiston. *The Granite Garden: Urban Nature and Human Design.* New York: Basic Books, 1984. A study of nature in the city.

Thayer, Robert L., Jr. *Gray World, Green Heart: Technology, Nature, and the Sustainable Landscape.* New York: John Wiley & Sons, 1994. A valuable philosophical examination of different attitudes toward technology and landscapes.

Thompson, William Irwin. *Gaia: A New Way of Knowing: Political Implications of the New Biology.* Great Barrington, Mass.: Lindisfarne Press, 1987. Examines the cultural implications of Gaia theory.

_____, ed. *Gaia 2: Emergence: The New Science of Becoming.* Hudson, N.Y.: Lindisfarne Press, 1991. Explores the significance of self-organizing systems.

Tibbs, Hardin. "Industrial Ecology: An Environmental Agenda for Industry." *Whole Earth Review,* no. 77 (winter 1992). Absolutely critical contribution to the emerging paradigm of industrial ecology, which calls for nothing less than the redesign of our industrial system so that pollution is eliminated and materials throughput and energy use are minimized.

Todd, Nancy Jack, and John Todd. *From Eco-Cities to Living Machines: Principles of Ecological Design.* Berkeley: North Atlantic Books, 1994. An eloquent exploration of ecological design principles. Examples include aquaculture, living machines, urban farming, and bioshelters. Essential reading.

Van der Ryn, Sim. *The Toilet Papers.* Sausalito, Calif.: Ecological Design Press, 1995. A detailed discussion of composting toilets.

Van der Ryn, Sim, and Peter Calthorpe. *Sustainable Communities: A New Design Synthesis for Cities, Suburbs, and Towns.* San Francisco: Sierra Club Books, 1991. A collection of essays on ecological design at town and city scales.

Waldrop, M. Mitchell. *Complexity: The Emerging Science at the Edge of Order and Chaos.* New York: Simon & Schuster, 1992. A history of complex-systems research at the Santa Fe Institute.

Wells, Malcolm. *Gentle Architecture.* New York: McGraw-Hill, 1981. A delightful examination of low-impact building techniques.

Wilson, Edward O. *The Diversity of Life.* Cambridge: Harvard Univ. Press, 1992. A passionate account of the emergence of biodiversity on Earth and the prospects for its maintenance.

_____, ed. *Biodiversity.* Washington, D.C.: National Academy Press, 1988. A collection of essays on the theme of biodiversity, with particular emphasis on policy issues.

World Commission on Environment and Development. *Our Common Future.* New York: Oxford Univ. Press, 1987. A key text in the north-south sustainability dialogue.

Worldwatch Institute. *State of the World.* Washington, D.C.: Worldwatch Institute. An annual wrap-up of the latest trends and statistics in environmental issues. Very informative.

Worster, Donald. *The Wealth of Nature: Environmental History and the Ecological Imagination.* New York: Oxford Univ. Press, 1993. Important collection of essays on environmental history and sustainability.

# INDEX

## About the Authors

Sim Van der Ryn is chairman and chief designer of the Ecological Design Institute, a nonprofit organization integrating design services, education, and research to build sustainability. A professor emeritus of architecture at the University of California, Berkeley, he was California State Architect and director of the state Office of Appropriate Technology in the 1970s. His other books include *Sustainable Communities* (Sierra Club, 1986) and *The Toilet Papers* (Ecological Design Press, reprinted 1995).

Stuart Cowan received his Ph.D. in complex systems from the University of California, Berkeley. He is a freelance ecological designer and writer in the San Francisco Bay Area and has worked on sustainability curricula ranging from elementary school through the university level.